Choosing the Win-Win Playground

Still Alive and Still Choosing Love:

Six Healthy Habits
for Positive Change

Sarah Day, OTL, CST-T, MPH

A Commitment to Shared Care

By choosing this book, you are doing more than supporting an author.

You are *stepping* into a larger ecosystem of care.

Twenty percent of net profits from this book are donated to the Win-Win Playground Foundation, helping expand access to group healing and educational experiences.

No additional action is required.
No extra giving is expected.

Simply by engaging with this work, you are participating in a model where creativity, wellness, and service are held together—without depletion, without hierarchy, and without leaving anyone behind.

Thank you for being here.
Thank you for choosing the Win-Win Playground.

Author's Invitation

"Believe in a love that is being stored up for you like an inheritance, and have faith that in this love there is a strength and a blessing so large that you can travel as far as you wish without having to step outside it."
—— **Rainer Maria Rilke, Letters to a Young Poet**

This book is about the journey of aging while choosing to play in the playground of wellness.

My hope is that as you engage with the Six Healthy Habits that follow, curiosity and wonder begin to blossom. That this book invites each of you who feels called to enter these pages to look inward rather than outward for the new way that will emerge for you.

It is a guide to showing up in love, letting go of outcome, and becoming a bigger, brighter ball of light on the planet—in a way that is personal, authentic, and just right for you. It is an invitation to follow your bliss, and let your joyful radiance fuel your creative projects with greater ease.

This book is also about learning how to serve the people we love without harming ourselves—or them—in the process.

Over the past thirty years, I have worked as a facilitator of health through my roles as an Occupational Therapist, CranialSacral Therapist and Teacher of Energy Systems. Throughout that time, I have dedicated a significant amount of energy on my own self work—to gently invite unhealthy, unconscious patterns into my awareness so they can shift into a matrix of greater health. I have come to understand these patterns as part of the *shadow*—the aspects of ourselves that live outside conscious awareness and tend to surface when we are stressed, afraid, or disconnected.

As these shadow patterns come into awareness, they do not disappear. What changes is our relationship to them. We gain the ability to notice them, soften around them, and choose a more supportive way forward.

The shadow does not only contain what we judge as "negative." Many of us also learned, early in life, to tuck away our light—our creativity, joy, confidence, and natural radiance—in order to fit in and feel safe. I refer to this hidden brilliance as the *golden shadow*.

As we engage in our self work with curiosity and compassion, the golden shadow begins to emerge. We reconnect with our creative essence, our agency, and our capacity to express ourselves fully in the world. This is the part of us that longs to be lived—not perfectly, but authentically.

Through this process, we begin to connect more deeply to the God-spark within—our individuated core essence—as equal members of the matrix of love and freedom that lives in us all.

This is not a book about being perfect, nor is it a guide to digging up trauma and throwing it away. There is wisdom in our trauma. When met with love and curiosity, it becomes a doorway rather than a burden. Our motivation for making change in the world is fueled both by what externally activates us—*signaling* that something does not feel right—and by our internal, authentic drive to be a bigger, brighter beacon of love on the planet.

I hope this book serves as a guide to support your connection to your deep, authentic self—so that, in full receivership of God's love and grace, you can more clearly discern what is right for you.

May you learn to accept and use the wisdom of those who came before you when it resonates in your body, and may you gently tune out the negative noise amplified by those who choose to play in less healthy playgrounds. This is a guide for shifting from valuing external authority to trusting your own inner guidance, from a place of equal connection to the Whole.

One of the life practices I return to often is pausing, taking a breath, and asking: *How can I support my life—and the lives of those around me—to be even more amazing than they already are?*

This book is my response to that question. It is a co-creation between my lived experience and the message that divine love and grace wish to bring forward at this time. In writing it—and in being vulnerable and open with you—I am practicing what I teach: showing up in love and letting go of outcome.

Throughout this book, I have used the words "God," "matrix of love and freedom," and "Universal Energy Field" interchangeably to describe a presence greater than ourselves. I invite you to interpret these words in whatever way resonates most deeply with your own personal beliefs. You may substitute Love, Higher Power, Infinite Intelligence, or simply the God of your own understanding. My intention is not to define a specific religious doctrine, but to point toward a source of guidance and connection that honors your unique spiritual path and perspective.

For me, God is not as an abstract concept. It is a lived, embodied experience. I feel it in my tissues as I participate in the Matrix of Love and Freedom that surrounds us all.

As a practicing Episcopalian and a somatic practitioner, I pray regularly, *"Let Thy will be done."* As I sit with this prayer, I open to spaciousness in my body and allow the flow of grace in and through me. As a CranioSacral Therapist, I envision my hands connected to my heart, filling with white and gold light, in service to the highest good of my client, and honor that in the Win-Win Playground of equality, both my field and my client's field will be nourished and supported at the end of the session.

In my experience, this relationship with God does not live only in prayer or professional service—it lives in the body. It expresses itself through creativity, play, and the willingness to participate fully in life without attachment to outcome. As I have learned to trust this embodied connection, it has invited me into forms of expression that once felt inaccessible or unsafe.

Since joining the Barbara Brennan School of Healing, I have shifted long-held feelings of "not enough"—especially connected to being the one person in my family growing up who was not a naturally gifted visual artist—and began painting for myself.

I moved through fears around public speaking and performed stand-up comedy for an audience of about one hundred people. I wrote and led a song circle and felt the flow of God moving through me in the playground of creation. I did all of this despite being mildly tone-deaf. I embraced the beauty of participation without attachment to mastery.

The likelihood of me ever becoming a professional singer is close to zero—and I love to sing. I am finding ways to do so in community that fit who I am. This, to me, is health. This is wellness.

In January 2025, another creative process unfolded. I looked at my life and said, *I don't choose to live this way.*

This realization arose not primarily because of my husband, but because my adult children—then nineteen and twenty-two—were still living at home and driving me crazy. I would set limits and make requests such as, "I am fifty-four. I deserve my own bathroom. Please use the hall bathroom," and those requests would be ignored. It felt like I was living in a dysfunctional frat house.

With the loving intention that my actions improve the quality of my relationships with each member of my family, I moved out. I rented a home a ten-minute walk away for four months.

The space this *intentional* action created—in my own life, and in the household I stepped away from—was *extraordinary*. Each morning, I made time for myself. I got to know myself not as mother, wife, or therapist, but as the curious, confident, loving, creative Sarah I had forgotten over time. By removing the constant noise of family, pets, and chores, I shifted from externally referencing to internally referencing. I became aware of—and shifted—subtle co-dependent patterns that had developed when my children were young and were persisting as we moved into adult-to-adult relationships.

When I returned home in May, I asked myself: *How can I make my life—and the lives of those I love—even better?*

I found Terry Real's Relational Therapy and began working with Lori Irwin of Lovescape.us. My husband and I gained tools to become better communicators. We shifted from complaint to request with each other and our adult children. We recommitted to each other and chose to navigate this dance of life as a team—playing in the Win-Win Playground, where we and those around us are nourished and have exactly what they need. We show up in love and let go of outcome. We encourage each other's creative projects. To me, this is wellness in relationship.

Each January, I begin working on a creative project. Even though I took a year off from formal study with the Barbara Brennan School of Healing this year, the rhythm of creation continues.

I hope you enjoy reading this book as much as I have enjoyed writing it.

With love,

Sarah

How To Use This Book

This book is not meant to be read only once, nor is it meant to be consumed quickly.

It is a companion.

You may choose to read it straight through, allowing the concepts, stories, and practices to gently layer themselves into your awareness. Or you may feel called to open to a specific page, chapter, or habit—trusting that whatever draws your attention is what your system is ready to receive.

There is no right way to use this book.

You may find that some sections resonate deeply while others create discomfort, resistance, or even irritation. These responses are information. They are invitations to pause, soften your gaze, and notice what is happening in your body, emotions, and thoughts. Nothing here is meant to be forced.

This book is experiential.

As you read, I invite you to slow down.
Notice your breath.

Notice sensation in your body.

Notice when you feel expansion—and when you feel contraction.

If you encounter a passage that feels energizing, consider reading it aloud. Let the words move through your tissues, not just your intellect. If something feels overwhelming, step away. Return to Breath. Try the Ho'oponopono practice described in Habit #3. Go for a walk. Drink water. Whatever you choose to do that is right for you, return when your system feels resourced.

The **Healthy Habits** introduced here are not checkboxes to complete. They are living practices designed to work together. You may find yourself leaning more heavily into one habit during certain seasons of life, and another during different seasons. This is natural.

You are encouraged to revisit chapters as your awareness grows.

The stories shared—including my own and Jorgia's—are offered not as prescriptions, but as mirrors. Take what resonates. Leave what does not. Your inner wisdom knows how to sort what is useful from what is not—if you allow it space to speak.

This book is not a replacement for medical care, mental health support, or professional guidance. It is an invitation to reconnect with your **agency**, your **body wisdom**, and your **direct relationship with God's love and grace**, alongside whatever forms of support are right for you.

Most importantly, remember this:

You are not broken.

You are not behind.

You are not failing.

You are learning how to choose—again and again—the play-ground that nourishes life.

Let this book support you in returning, gently and repeatedly, to the **Win-Win Playground**—where you and the whole are held in equal care.

This is not a book to finish.
It's a book to return to—
each time with softer eyes.

Contents

Introduction

On Christmas Eve 2025, while visiting my in-laws in Sacramento, California for the holidays, I woke at five in the morning with a searing pain across my abdomen and knew something was very wrong. By six a.m., my loving husband and son had our insurance sorted and had me safely delivered to the hospital. By one p.m., I was in surgery. By four p.m., I was in recovery from a ruptured colon and an abdominal abscess. One of my kidneys was in renal failure.

That first night in the hospital, I woke with a heavy pressure on my chest and a deep internal knowing that I was standing at a precipice. It felt as though I had a choice—to leave or to stay. I chose to stay. I chose life.

My next clear memory is of a larger-than-life African American woman seated beside my bed, wearing a wide black Victorian gown. Her calm presence filled the room. I have come to call her the Spirit of Sutter. Thank you, Ma'am, for creating a safe space for healing—and for the co-creative endeavor with the Divine that flowed through me on my final day in the hospital and became this book.

This book is dedicated to all of us who are interested in playing in the Win-Win Playground of life.

I hold deep gratitude for the entire staff at Sutter Hospital and for the four roommates who shared my thirteen-day healing journey. Witnessing your processes expanded my understanding of the beauty contained within the vastness of human experience. I am also deeply grateful for my family, friends, and facilitator colleagues in the Upledger CranioSacral and Barbara Brennan School of Healing communities, who surrounded me with love as I chose to live fully—richly connected to the Matrix of Love and Freedom that surrounds us all. The concept of being "one up" or "one down" comes from Terry Real's *The New Rules of Marriage* . This book builds on that lineage by weaving in the framework of the Human Energy Field, as described by Barbara Brennan in her books *Hands of Light* and *Core Light Healing*. Together, these perspectives expand Terry Real's relational grid—one up/one down, walled off/boundaryless—beyond our partnerships and into our relationship with the Whole: The Universal Energy Field that nourishes and sustains us. Although what I see when I work with my clients matches what Barbara Brennan describes in her books above, I have chosen to use the term "personal energy field" throughout this book instead of "Human Energy Field".

In these pages, I describe four playgrounds: the Win-Win Playground, the Masochist Playground, the Competitive Playground, and the Human Grenade Playground. Each playground represents an energetic matrix—a field of energy with distinct qualities and patterns.

My hope is that, as you read, you deepen your sense of personal agency. As you become more aware of which energetic playground you are engaging in, you regain choice. You step into a playground when your internal environment shifts. It is your automatic stress responses that bring you into the maladaptive matrices of the Masochist, Competitive and Human Grenade Playgrounds. It is awareness, breath, and engaging with the Six Healthy Habits for Positive Change described in this book that will support you to realign to the Win-Win Playground. Throughout the book, I will invite you to look inward, offering pauses, reflection prompts, and gentle resets. The change begins within.

In this game of life, each of us has opportunities to explore all four playgrounds for learning and soul evolution. I invite you to hold yourself in compassion as you explore the playgrounds and the internal habits that may keep you anchored in a particular playground. Each one affects the personal energy field in specific ways—and, over time, influences our tissues and our health.

Your sense of agency and your ability to choose the qualities of life you want to cultivate increases as you shed your attachment to the ways the world sees you and deepen your connection to your authentic wise adult self. As you become aware of the playground dynamics within you and around you—and as you assess whether your current playground is sustainably nourishing you—you access choice.

You get to say **"no"** to patterns of depletion and separation.

You get to say **"yes"** to patterns of nourishment and expansion.

You get to say **"yes"** to stepping into the Win-Win Playground.

Once you step into the Win-Win Playground, you are not finished. In times of stress and low resource, we all move into the maladaptive playgrounds. It is the amount of time we spend in these playgrounds that changes. With awareness, our time in these playgrounds become clearer and shorter. Our vertical movement from a stressed to a calm, heart centered state becomes easier. We start to develop a life of showing up for ourselves and the whole equally, connecting with kindness while letting go of outcome. It is a life of feeling the nourishing energies of the Earth and God's love meeting your own spark of creativity and passion to feed the changes that want to be made in ourselves and the world.

From that place of love and connection we get to ask, *"What is mine to do?"*

As more of us become aware, more of us can actively choose to live in the Win-Win Playground—fully supported by the planet and by God's love and grace in our lives.

"Our entire reason for being on Earth is to love. Nothing else matters but love."

—John Paul. <u>The Telepathy Tapes Podcast.</u>

Healthy Habit #1
Showing Up in Love, Softening Our Gaze, Letting Go of Outcome

Showing Up In Love

What does being creative mean to you?

Take a moment to reflect.

We create in countless ways throughout our lives. Each time we pause and step out of habitual patterns of thought and behavior, we are creating a new way of being.

Most of us carry ideas about projects we want to engage in—personal growth projects, home projects, artistic projects, professional endeavors, and initiatives we hope will make the world a better place.

Regardless of the form our creative work takes, creation for positive change naturally emerges when our wise adult self is in relationship with our core essence and with the nourishing field of Love and Freedom that surrounds us. If we are in a depletion pattern—where we are sending out more energy than we are receiving—our creative flow can become blocked.

Most of us are familiar with this experience. We move into effort, there is tightening in our tissues, and we may become fixated on a particular outcome. Often our internal motivator, starts spewing some pretty negative self-talk, sending us into a procrastination pattern. In this stressed state, we can lose touch with what is actually happening in our environment, and start seeing the world through the lens of our younger, wounded child eyes. We often lose sight of the big picture and become overly focused on minute details. We lose sight of the forest by focusing too intensely on the trees.

Shifting from a blocked creative state to healthy creative flow can be challenging. And the bigger the creative impact has on your ability to tune into your golden shadow aspects—your agency, power, beauty, and capacity to be a bright beacon of love in the world—the bigger the block can be.

Ease of healthy creativity occurs when we are connected to our wise adult self and there is a balance between receiving from the Matrix of Love that surrounds us and internal flow, as well as a balance between the energies of our upper chakras and our lower chakras.

Whether you are an experienced energy practitioner and familiar with the personal energy field, or this is absolutely new to you,

you will experience this blocked flow either through your body's felt sense of tightness, your emotional charge, or through the poor quality of your mental clarity around your creative project.

Most of us only notice this balance of our energetic system once we've already lost it. I will be giving examples of how our energetic systems go out of alignment in Habit #2, when I describe the Four Playgrounds. As you read about the energetic imbalances in each of the three maladaptive playgrounds, I hope you develop increased insight about your own patterns of imbalance, so you can make the conscious choice to come back to love, to centered receiving, and positive flow as you choose the Win-Win Playground.

Attuning to the quality of the energetic balance in our lives and recentering when we move out of balance is the lived experience of *Showing Up in Love.*

***

Throughout this book, I will return again and again to a simple five-part practice that helps clear the internal restriction patterns that decrease the flow of your life force. For now, simply begin by noticing when your tissues tighten and when you are moving out of centered alignment— and experiment with responding with love rather than judgment.

Creating a healthy matrix of love within you is the first of the five-part practice introduced in Habit #3. As you begin to notice how your habitual ways of striving, thinking and dealing with stress effect your chakra and balance system, set the intention that you are holding yourself in the healthiest container of love that you are able to be with in this moment. As you participate in the somatic exercises in this book, notice how your capacity to hold a stronger and healthier container of love for yourself increases, even as you find yourself out of alignment. It is our capacity to hold a healthy flow of love for ourselves, even in times of stress, that helps us be present enough to identify that we have moved out of alignment and return to center.

When you are in effort, you may notice your body pushed forward from center. If you are in overwhelm, you may notice your body pushed backwards from center. If you are too focused on details and self-critical, your body maybe tilted to the left, if you are off in daydreaming and fantasy, your body may be tilted to the right, if you are over intellectualizing your energy will be up, if you are caught in self-absorbed passion, your energy will be down.

When we move out of centered alignment, our chakra system becomes imbalanced, restricting the nourishing flow of bio-plasma into our personal energy field. Once you are aware, you can place your hand on your heart, take a breath, and honoring what is coming up into your awareness, invite your energy fields back to centered alignment. We can open fully to receive the energies of love and freedom in a balanced way—often in just a breath or two.

***

Take a moment to notice your breath. Then say to yourself:

I invite my energy field into centered alignment and balanced receiving of love.

Take another breath. Notice any changes that occur in your awareness as you invite your energy field into the centered alignment and balanced receiving of love that occurs in the Win-Win Playground. The changes may be large or small. All are okay.

Whether your change-making unfolds through the arts, environmental justice, education, parenting, community organizing, or the healing arts, the act of creating something new asks the same thing of us:

Alignment with the highest good within ourselves *and* with the highest good of the whole.

When we align with our highest good *and* the highest good of the whole, our personal energy field automatically starts moving toward balance.

I invite you to quietly say to yourself:

I am setting the intention to align to my highest good and the highest good of the whole.

***

Take a moment to feel how the intention to connect to this alignment affects your tissues, emotions and thoughts. This is about possibility, not success or failure.

Energy follows intention. Your intention is your agency. You have the agency to feed the qualities you want to support in your life. One possible quality to feed is *ease and positive flow.* To support these qualities growing in all aspects of your life, you can say:

I am opening to the possibility of being in ease and positive flow with my creative projects.

***

At this point, pause; notice how your body softens, your emotions settle and your mind clears. Take a moment to focus on your heart. Imagine the armor you have created around your heart softening and falling away. Perceive the flow of energy moving up your spine into your heart, however it is right for you to perceive this energy. Our closest, largest source of love energy is from the Earth. Take a moment, to be here, now. Tune into what your soul's desire is for you to create, and let the love from the crystalline core of the Earth flow up into your heart.

When we set the intention to be in ease of positive flow, we can choose the next right action from a place of loving connection to Heaven and Earth. Some people experience these shifts as sensations, some as images, and some simply as a sense of ease or clarity—there is no right way to perceive this. For those of you who are visual, the energetic intentional line is a yellow line that runs up and down the spine all the way up to infinity, and all the way down to the center of the Earth. The lines also run through our limbs.

Barbara Brennan called this line the Hara. For the purpose of this book, I will call this energetic line that flows into our chakra system and physical body the intentional energetic line. Dr John E. Upledger—the founder of Upledger CranioSacral Therapy—saw this energy system in the body and decided to call it Vertices. He found that when making tissue changes, it was important to tune into the Vertices system at the end of a session to support the changes made in the tissues in this field for quicker recovery. Our energy fields and our tissues are intimately connected, supporting flow in both our bodies and our personal energy field are important for the practice of *Showing Up in Love*.

Softening Our Gaze

Years ago, when I began my training as a CranioSacral Therapist, I started noticing subtle but consistent shifts in my own body when I moved out of alignment. When my attention drifted from my heart up into my head while working with a client, the energy around my eyes would become intense. I would lean forward slightly, and the pressure in my hands would grow heavier as I engaged with the client's tissues.

These were early signals of separation.

In those moments, I was no longer serving as a facilitator of my client's path to health. The work shifted from listening to fixing, from presence to effort, and from trust to control. The love flowing through my heart into my hands became less neutral. Instead, my mind had taken the lead—quietly deciding what change should look like and attempting to make it happen.

Softening the gaze is a way back.

I have two favorite ways of softening the tension around my eyes, both courtesy Donna Eden's teachings on eye health. The first is called palming—rub your palms together vigorously until they create heat. Then place your warm palms over your closed eyes for 30 seconds to decrease tension. Breath slowly as you allow the muscles around your eyes to soften. You may also notice your heart rate decreasing as you relax.

The second method is called butterfly kisses. This technique involves very softly pinching the skin in a circular motion around each eye. (Imagine your fingers are butterfly feet- the pinching should be barely perceptible. Soft pinches to the skin are extremely effective in relaxing muscles. As you pinch, you are releasing tension around the nerve endings traveling through the fascia right below the skin. This creates a reflexogenic effect, which means that the relaxation in the nerve travels backwards toward any muscles it innervates as well as throughout the nervous system.

When we soften our eyes, we soften our bodies. We release the forward lean, the grasping pressure, the subtle urgency to intervene. We return to the heart as the organizing center and allow healing and creativity to emerge. From this place, love and grace move freely, the armoring around our heart softens, and our ability to create positive change increases both within us and around us.

This is the practice at the heart of Habit #1: noticing when we tighten, and choosing—again and again—to soften and return to heart centered alignment.

Letting Go of Outcome

When we show up in love, release attachment to outcome, and trust right timing, what unfolds is often far more beautiful than anything our limited perspective could have planned.

In therapeutic and co-creative environments, we step into a shared field of knowing. We align with the highest good of the individual and the whole, holding an open, centered, flowing heart. In this space, the Higher Self—the part of us that is already whole and resourced—meets the present self and the past self, including both wounded and joyful aspects. Together, they reveal the next step toward healing.

Co-creation happens as our Higher Self aligns in service to the highest good of all. From this shared field, our understanding of health, creativity, and possibility expands—supported by love and grace that are always present.

We become clear, sustainable positive change makers when unconscious fixations move into conscious awareness—when we shift from separation into connection. When we are caught in separation, our sense of what is possible becomes constrained by past wounds. Our memories—and the expectations of outcome that emerges from those memories—limit our ability to connect fully to the matrix of love and freedom surrounding us. We create energetic armor in our personal energy field that restricts the flow of Grace into our lives.

Even anticipation can limit positive change. When we expect a dramatic event to occur, but the changes unfolding are subtle and profound, disappointment causes us to miss the transformation taking place—in our lives and in the creative projects with which we engage.

I like the terms *The Slow Train* and *The Fast Train* to positive change. I had a Fast Train experience after participating in my first CranioSacral Dolphin class in the Bahamas with Integrative Intentions. During the dolphin swim portion of the class, the dolphins gave me the gift of opening my third-eye chakra. Photos from this time can be seen on my website and clearly show a dark blue light surrounding my head.

I hold deep gratitude for this gift. And yet, the following year was one of the most challenging of my life. I began seeing ghosts and even had them waking me in the middle of the night to communicate. That year, I worked closely with my healing team to support my system in regaining agency—learning to reset my boundaries so that I was in control of what I was perceiving and what energies were allowed into my field.

I am grateful both for the gift I received from the dolphins and for the support that emerged around me during that time. And still, as I continue to live in relationship with the energy of ease and positive flow, I can say I prefer the Slow Train—the path of subtle but profound change in my life.

That said, the creative project of this book is clearly on the Fast Train. As I work on it, I am showing up in love—sensing deeply into my heart coherence as I write. I soften the stiff gaze created by anticipation about how the book will be received, while also taking grounded, practical steps to create a professional-level work. I balance this effort with deep trust—"Thy will be done"—knowing that this book will reach exactly the number of people meant to read it.

Over-attachment to a specific outcome can lock the creative process entirely. It is natural to dream of a better life for yourself and for those around you. And I encourage you not to become too fixated on a particular dream. Our dreams evolve as we soften the armor that limits our access to the true beauty of the world in which we live.

As our lens of possibility widens, our dreams will change. One simple practice that supports detachment from outcome is adding the phrase "or something even better" to your images of the future.

A Call to Action

If you find yourself feeling stuck, pause. Reconnect with the matrix of love and freedom surrounding us. Soften your armor and invite in Grace. Tune into your core essence and feel the golden spark of the part of you that is God, and the part of God that is you in every cell in your body. Open yourself to the possibility that a Plan B—something far greater than you can currently imagine—is waiting to emerge. When it emerges, say yes!

The universal energy field of love and freedom is already supporting you. The flow of grace is all around you. Your role is to receive.

I invite you to receive these words not only with your mind, but with the wisdom of your tissues. Breathe. Allow their frequency to move through your body. Notice any fixated ideas about how life—or the world—should be, and gently allow them to soften.

Align your intention with ease and positive flow. Step into the Win-Win playground. Trust that what is meant for you will arrive when the timing is right—for your highest good and the highest good of the whole.

Healthy Habit #2
Align to the Win-Win Playground

When I went into menopause, I began mouth-breathing. I knew enough about breath and its relationship to health to recognize that it was time to invest in myself more deeply if I wanted to stay on a path of wellness.

I consulted with a myofunctional therapist and an orthodontist and was told I would need gum surgery and six months in a palate expander. I did the myofunctional exercises, but as I checked in with my body wisdom, I decided to explore less invasive approaches before committing to surgery.

At the time, I was working as a CranioSacral Therapist and had witnessed profound changes in clients—especially in group, multi-hands healing environments. I signed myself up as a client for a five-day multi-hands program with Integrative Intentions.

Later in this book, I write about the complexities of healing. True to form, on day four of that first program, it became clear that my system was doing preparatory work—and that I would need a second five-day program to complete the shift. Thankfully, another program was already scheduled two weeks later at the Upledger Institute in Palm Beach, Florida. I signed up, flew to Florida, and repeated the process. On day four of that second program, I regained access to nasal breathing—and I still have it today.

During that second program, I felt called to ask my Higher Self: What is the purpose of suffering? The answer came back as a single word: **fun.**

I remember shouting, "That is not a helpful answer!"

When I returned home, I asked the question again—this time to a wise woman in my community. She said, "We choose the frequencies we want to play in. If we are suffering, some part of us is choosing to suffer." That didn't sit well with me either. It felt incomplete.

What I have come to understand over time is this: *when we become aware,* we get to choose which playing field we wish to engage.

There are four primary playgrounds:

- The Win-Win Playground — where both self and the whole are nourished and matter equally

- The Masochist Playground — where you believe consciously or unconsciously that others matter more than you

- The Competitive Playground — where you believe consciously or unconsciously that you matter more than others

- The Human Grenade Playground — where deep disconnection from love leads to harm of self and others

One of the most common limiting beliefs I encounter in my work is the idea that positive change requires sacrifice. When we unconsciously align with this belief, we may over-give, deplete ourselves, and slowly erode our health and vitality. Over time, this pattern undermines not only our well-being, but also our ability to serve in a sustainable way.

The Win-Win Playground offers a different orientation. Here, we make choices that support ourselves as equal participants in the whole—while also supporting the whole itself. When we live this way, health, creativity, and service arise together.

This is the foundation of becoming a Healthy Positive Change Maker.

The Energetic Landscape of Choice

As we move through life, energy is always doing one of two things:

- Flowing and nourishing (+)

- Contracting and depleting (–)

This is true both personally and collectively. When both the self and the whole are nourished, we are playing in the Win-Win Playground. When one is elevated at the expense of the other, imbalances emerge.

I have often heard it said that souls are lined up across time and space to come to Earth right now. There is a palpable excitement around this moment in history. I know that this can be hard to believe when you turn on the news. The news is showing us the world that is aligned with fear-based decisions. However, we, as humans, are doing a better job of supporting each other. At a planetary level, we are at a tipping point. More of us are stepping out of automatic, non-conscious survival patterns and making conscious choices to align with Love and Freedom. With awareness and agency, we are saying *no* to fear and *yes* to becoming co-creators with the Matrix of Love and Freedom to help shape a better world.

It is an extraordinary time to be alive. The number of people actively choosing to play in the Win-Win Playground is growing, and the sense of ease and flow accompanying this expansion of consciousness is truly wondrous. Collectively, we are aligning with love, kindness, and the sense that what is happening to others also affects us. We are declaring our collective "no" to the greed and fear based policies of our governments and "yes" to policies that support each human and the planet itself as equals within our ecosystem. As our external and internal energy fields become less separate, we actually move from reactivity to responsiveness. We are able to influence our outer world by choosing what to focus on in our inner world. We discern what is ours to do from a deep connection to our own inner wisdom and a deep connection to the whole from a centered experience of life.

When we notice our habitual patterns and pause, we regain access to choice. We can choose the Win-Win Playground. And when we align with it—while letting go of attachment to outcome—we open ourselves to the field of miracles, the field of wonder.

In doing so, we become the change we wish to see in the world.

We become Positive Change Makers.

And in that choice—made again and again—we remember who we are becoming.

The Four Energetic Playgrounds

Flowing and Nourishing Energy (+)

Contracting and Depleting Energy (-)

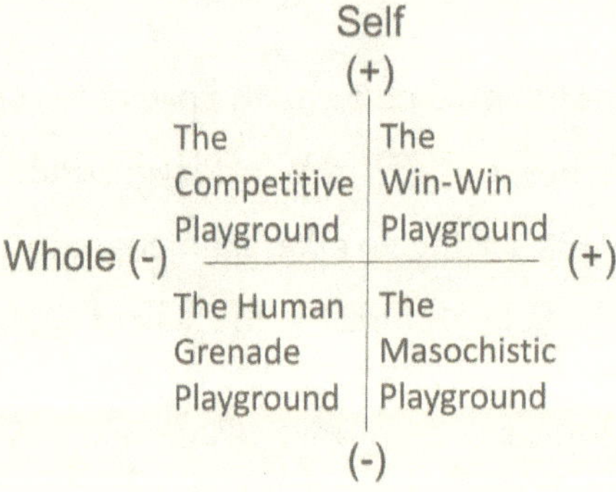

You don't need to stay in any playground forever.

Choice is always available.

The Win-Win Playground

Nourishing Ourselves and the Whole Equally

When we set the intention to step into the Win-Win Playground, we invite ease of positive flow into our lives. We make a conscious action to align our state of being with the highest good of ourselves and the whole. When we do this, we step into a new field of energy called a Matrix where we and everyone around us are equally nourished, supported and loved—often felt as more ease in the body and breath.

For me, this often begins as a subtle softening in my chest, an opening of breath and a deepening connection to my heart coherence. A sense of safety emerges, along with access to joy and the feeling that I don't need to rush. From this place, I trust that I will know the right action at the right divine time.

A week after I returned home from the hospital, a long-time client reached out, insisting that I work with her that week. I tuned in and checked the statement, "Working with this client this week is for my highest good and the highest good of all," and received a yes for both.

Normally, I would have panicked slightly. I knew I did not have the physical strength to stand for an hour and work as a CranioSacral Therapist with her physical body. Instead, I paused and connected with my heart coherence. I checked in with curiosity. I opted for Plan B.

As I aligned with the Win-Win Playground, where my needs and my client's needs were held with equal importance. I was able to negotiate a nourishing, win-win scenario that worked for both of us. I offered a phone consultation which she happily accepted and somatically guided her through her process.

It felt good to support her—and to support myself at the same time.

This is a good example of the Win-Win playing field in practice.

It is from this grounded presence that we become a beacon of light in the world. We nourish ourselves and those around us not only through what we do, but through who we are. What we do is the icing on the cake of the Win-Win Playground. When our actions are fueled by love rather than fear, we begin co-creating a reality that fully supports the qualities that we hold in high esteem—for ourselves and for all. In this way, we become powerful Positive Change Makers.

For many, the act of setting an intention **to open to the possibility** of stepping more fully into the Win-Win playground will be enough for positive change to start occurring inside and outside the body.

As you go for your daily walk, you can say: *I am open to the possibility of living more fully in the Win-Win Playground.*

This statement, or any statement that includes the words "I am open to the possibility..." both feeds energy into your grounded line of intention, bypasses fear responses that block change, and opens your lens of perception. You will start looking for and seeing ways the Win-Win playground is already around you, and as you notice the possibilities, you will begin interacting with your environment in a different, more nurturing way.

Stating the affirmation out loud, singing it, and saying it in your head while you walk, dance or move rhythmically also magnifies the power of the words and helps your tissues vibrationally absorb the new matrix energy.

A word of caution about affirmations. You will notice that I am **not** encouraging you to make the statement "I am living in the Win-Win Playground". A statement like this constricts the fluidity of life. It may also trick your tissues, into believing that your current life, which may actually have strong depletion, one-up/one-down, and disconnected patterns, *is* the Win-Win Playground.

Here is another example: many intuitive healers, struggle with finances. If they stand in front of the mirror and say "I am wealthy" as they are living in a tiny apartment, with loud neighbors and cockroaches, the right brain and the tissues can respond with, "okay, this is what wealth looks like", and no change occurs. By saying "I am open to the possibility of being wealthy", or better yet, "I am open to the possibility of having all my needs, and all of the needs of those around me met with ease", the possibility of movement and change increases in your life.

The Win-Win playground is all about you and those around you being on an equal valuation with respect to the whole. It is about balance, and opening ourselves to receive nurturance, both from our upper and lower chakras. The Earth is the largest physical object in our close vicinity and it has a consciousness and deep love for us. Take time to connect with the Earth, feel it's love flow into you through your feet and your root chakra. When I am open to receiving the highest love from the center of the Earth, I see a red light flow into my body and feel a softening in my tissues. The red light moves up from the root chakra at the base of my spine to the second chakra. It mixes with the orange light within my second chakra, the sacral chakra. The sacral chakra represents our personal love. When orange and red mix together we are energized to engage in the tasks in which we are authentically able to feel our love for ourselves. For me, this is walks with my family and dogs, bike riding and eating food grown and prepared with love.

There is a chemical alchemy that occurs when the golden light of your soul star joins with the orange-red light of your grounded self-love. This golden red-orange concoction becomes our purpose. It is the mixing of what we love with what we are good at, with where we are called to make change in our lives.

***

Take a moment to feel into the flow of this creative essence within you.

Sit with it for a while and continue when you are ready.

Following Our Bliss

The Dalai Lama has said that the purpose of life is to be happy. This is not happiness from external gratification. It is not saying yes to that second bowl of ice cream, but rather, seeking deep connection to the happiness that lives within each of us when we are authentically living connected to our internal light, and taking actions that are fed from that light. When this happiness is allowed to shine, happiness evolves into joy and bliss. When we follow our bliss—what brings us joy from the core of ourselves—happiness resonates in our tissues on a cellular level. I call these experiences blissed-in moments.

Being blissed-in is a state of embodiment and balanced connection to the energies of heaven and earth. It is different from being blissed-out. When we are blissed-out, we may have expansive, out-of-body experiences or moments of spiritual awakening. Our upper chakras may feel wide open—but the experience is disconnected from the heart and the lower chakras that anchor us to the Earth's here and now. Blissed-out states feel wonderful, which is one reason mind-altering substances persist in our culture. But they are not sustainable patterns for health, and can even lead to mental breakdowns.

Blissed-in experiences, on the other hand, are deeply nourishing. They arise when we are open to receiving from both Heaven and Earth while remaining fully embodied. As children, many of us accessed blissed-in states naturally—often through play, movement, or time in nature. Over time, many of us forget how to return to these moments.

A few years ago, I had a blissed-in moment while eating at Sorrel—a Michelin-starred restaurant in San Francisco. I actually screamed—I was so surprised by the experience—and the poor waiter rushed over to make sure I was okay. I started laughing and said, "This is the best thing I have ever eaten in my life!" If you're curious, it was a triple-fried sunchoke with fig compote. I encourage Sorrel to keep it on their menu!

Restaurants that consciously source and prepare their food—and pay their staff well—are aligning with the Win-Win Playground. Set an intention to seek out places like this in your own community. You may be surprised by what you find. Hidden gems are everywhere.

Our calls to action as positive change makers on this planet, are fueled by our rage—the discomfort that arises when we see the world stepping out of alignment with the Matrix of Love and Freedom, (I write about this in Habit #5), and through the creative projects that arise through following our bliss. At this point in your process of stepping into the Win-Win Playground, I encourage you to take some time to reflect on the things that bring you deep joy, and feed those things in your life.

As you open to living more fully in the Win-Win Playground, you will still find yourselves jumping into the other playgrounds. They are all around us, and are the playgrounds which our adapted child-self is familiar. I believe it is impossible to live fully in the world without interacting with them. The new way for all of us, is to see the parts of ourselves that have become the energetic pattern of each playground and to interact with these parts from a place of love and conscious awareness. Take a moment to honor yourself. The adaptations you made as a child were created to keep you safe within the less supportive energetic fields in which you were raised.

As we become adults and upgrade in to playing in healthier playgrounds, these early adapted safety strategies often no longer serve us. We can compassionately invite these younger separated parts of ourselves back into present connection, and allow our wise adult self to lead the way forward. In the Win-Win Playground, our wise adult self is the decision maker and finds new ways to use language, images and action to promote positive change.

The Energetic Framework of the Win-Win Playground

Playgrounds as Fields of Energy

A field of energy is called a matrix. Habitual matrices are created through consistent patterns in your internal and external environment. Your personal energy field is influenced by physical events, emotional experiences, your thoughts, your beliefs and the matrices with which you interact.

For example, if you grew up in an environment where it was normal not to know if you would have a next meal, you were raised in a matrix of scarcity. This was not a single event affecting your field; it was a way of life presented to you by your parents—and possibly your community—and it came with a complex spiritual belief system that was mostly non-conscious. The range of spiritual beliefs connected to a matrix of scarcity is vast and may vary from "original sin makes us unworthy of God's love and abundance" to "there is no God—we are on our own, so we better take what we can when we can."

As we age, we become more aware of the variety of matrices available to us. We begin to upgrade our spiritual belief systems, and shift into healthier matrices. For example, around ten years ago, I had a brief conversation with the parents of a young women who was attending a summer language emersion program with my oldest child. Her dad made the statement: "Life is amazing, and it keeps getting better."

As he made that statement, I had a "wow" moment. It struck me with a pretty significant amount of energy that I no longer spiritually believed the statement "life is amazing" to be true, and that realization made me sad. In the weeks that followed, his words stayed with me, and I began to recognize that while I had experienced moments where "life was amazing," my overall life had resonated with a matrix of struggle. I was not living in the matrix of "life is amazing," and I realized I wanted to.

I grew up with severe social anxiety and sensory processing challenges that made going to school difficult. My younger brother had severe dyslexia and difficulties with emotional regulation, which made our home life stressful as well. I built a career supporting families with children who have special needs, which kept me immersed in that matrix of stress. I also chose to adopt a child with special needs, creating a home environment similar to the one in which I was raised.

I allowed myself to wonder, what would it be like to spiritually believe "Life is amazing, and it keeps getting better"? That sense of wonder softened my field and allowed it to shift.

I opened a private practice and started attracting adult clients who resonated with "life is amazing"—people who had been generally healthy and successful throughout their lives and were seeking support in expanding their capacity to follow their bliss. I supported them on their journeys and learned from them. Work became fun and playful.

Over time, "life is amazing" became my reality matrix. I consciously began interacting with the Win-Win Playground. Now I say "yes" to amazing experiences, such as exploring places like Antarctica and South Georgia and standing in a field of 200,000 king penguins. I explore the beauty of the world while writing books that are meaningful and supportive to myself and others, and I gift a percentage of the profits to charity. I facilitate group programs that support each participant to connect with their deep knowing selves so they are able to shift to wellness in the way that is right for them. I commit energy to support a healing center that honors each individuals path to wellness. I regularly have date nights with my husband and have conversations with him about how we can make our lives amazing together. I work with my learning edge on how to request my needs in a healthy way while I listen fully to the needs of those I love, and play with creative kindness.

This is the Win-Win Playground.

Our Personal Energetic Fields

Several years ago, while working as a facilitator of authentic connection and health in my role as a CranioSacral Therapist, I began seeing the energy fields around my clients as I worked. This happened most clearly during multi-hands sessions, and at times the light I perceived was so bright it was blinding. I saw opalescent flowing light enter the body, as the client opened to the flow of Grace and allowed Grace to make vibrational changes on a cellular level.

When I first began seeing this opalescent light in action, the brightness was painful to my eyes. I realized I needed guidance and training, and I enrolled in the Barbara Brennan School of Healing, as what I was experiencing aligned with what Barbara Brennan described in her book *Hands of Light*.

The painful, overwhelming experience did not disappear immediately. As I continued precepting Advanced CranioSacral Therapy classes and retreats, I often needed to take breaks—to close my eyes, drink water, and ask for guidance.

One day, a colleague shared an insight that stayed with me: that much of our armoring comes from our inability to be with the true beauty of the world. I began intentionally opening to that beauty in a healthier way. This shift did not happen overnight—It unfolded slowly over the next year.

The result is that now, I often see a golden grid around myself and my clients. I perceive this as the Matrix of God's Love and Freedom that connects us all. I see the individual golden grids of each of our seventh-level fields, which—along with the sixth-level opalescent light of divine love—represent the matrix system in our field. I see opalescent waves of light entering the body—what I understand as Grace in action—creating cellular changes beyond what our human minds can fully comprehend.

When a client first begins connecting with the field of Grace, their armor can initially block its flow, and the light may appear frenetic. I now understand that it was this frenetic quality that my eyes once found so painful.

To support my clients in receiving Grace more fully, when I see this pattern, I consciously hold my own sixth-level field of divine love and grace in coherence. This supports their process without my needing to do anything to them. My field becomes a model for a different way of being—one that allows Grace to flow with more ease.

This feels deeply nourishing in my own tissues. I am supporting my highest good while also supporting my client's highest good. This, to me, is wellness in action—playing in the energies of the Win-Win Playground.

Barbara Brennan worked as a physicist at NASA, before she opened her School of Healing. She described a field of bio-plasma that surrounds us all as the Universal Energy Field. According to her model, the bio-plasma feeds and nourishes us through our chakra system. The Bible states that the consciousness of God is omnipresent, and it makes sense to me that God—Love—is present in every molecule of bio-plasma moving into us. The primary purpose of this nourishment is to support our emotional system, the structural systems of our body and personal energy field, and our individuated creativity through our actions.

The bio-plasma comes into our chakra system with the neutral consciousness of love. As it moves through the chakras, it is transformed into different frequencies to support our physical body as well as the various levels of our personal energy field. The bio-plasma supports who we are in each moment and what we need for survival.

If our nervous system has moved into overwhelm and our automatic survival systems are activated, the bio-plasma will feed and energize the survival strategy present in that moment. If we are calm, present, and aware, the bio-plasma has the opportunity to support the expression of love we wish to bring into the world through our actions, words, art, and intentions. In this way, our chakra system supports us by nourishing the state we are in at each moment.

Changes in our personal energy field and body occur through intentional awareness. As we become aware of this process, we can actively and consciously choose the energies we want to cultivate. When aligned with the Win-Win Playground, we choose to nourish energies such as equality, kindness, safety, curiosity, wonder, and generosity as creative forces. As we open to trust in the whole—and thereby open to receive fully in a balanced way—positive change in our lives begins to expand exponentially in the areas we choose to feed.

Carl Jung offers the analogy of a tiny island in a vast ocean to describe the relationship between our conscious awareness of our belief patterns compared to the unconscious psyche. As we begin the journey of reconnecting with our deep, authentic selves, we expand our awareness of who we are. We widen our lens of perception and gain agency through the process of becoming the person we long to be by feeding the energy of the positive traits with which we align.

It can be easier to see positive traits in others than in ourselves. Before we move into an introduction to the chakra system, I invite you to participate in this exercise with me.

***

Take a moment to think of someone in your community that you admire. Name the qualities of that person that truly stand out to you. It may be unrestrained laughter, compassion, generosity, positivity, or commitment to a cause.

Feel into your body's response to the positive traits you have just named. Your body's response may be light and flowing or dense and stuck—it doesn't matter— dense and stuck energy simply means you have more armoring around your golden shadow self. Take a moment to hold yourself in a bubble of love and soften any armor that is presenting.

The qualities that you strongly see and admire in others are the same qualities that exist in your golden shadow. This is your core essence. You only notice and have a strong reaction to the qualities in others that also exist in yourself. Within your core essence is your incredible capacity to love, laugh, persevere, create, and innovate—qualities that are ready to emerge in your life.

Your core essence feeds your intentional body, and your intentional body feeds your chakra system. Your chakra system feeds your personal energy field and physical body. When we set the intention to show up in love, soften our gaze, and let go of outcome, we choose to engage in our human experience with curiosity and wonder. Our core essence, our guides, and our journey into accepting that it is okay to follow our bliss will guide us.

Introduction to the Chakra System

As I present this model of the chakra system, take time to feel your experience of it. Throughout this book, I emphasize the importance of internal referencing. Your lived experience of your chakra system is more valuable than the model presented here. If you have difficulty sensing this system, I invite you to engage your imagination and allow images to emerge from your deep, authentic self—images that can inform you in the way that is just right for you at this time.

In the model I am describing, the core essence of each person feeds the energetic intention line which has seven main points where chakras emerge. There are two single chakras: the root chakra and the crown chakra. The root chakra, or first chakra, originates at the base of the spine at the coccygeal-sacral joint and opens downwards towards the center of the earth. The root chakra regulates the first of the structured fields in your personal energy field—the etheric field. The crown chakra, or seventh chakra, originates at the top of the head and opens upward toward the sky. Chakras two through six are paired chakras, with one cone in the front of the body and the other in the back.

***

I invite you to take a moment to tune into your sense of how your root chakra and crown chakra are connected and working together to support your personal energy field. Take some time to be with the two poles of your chakra system with curiosity and love. You might ask yourself:

How do these chakras shift as I consciously align to the Win-Win

Playground and allow myself to be nourished by the balanced energies of Heaven and Earth, as an equal member of the whole?

Take a moment to feel into the shift that occurs with this alignment.

Remaining in this state of imagination and awareness, move up your spine from the root chakra to the front of the joint where the sacrum meets the lumbar spine. This is the location where the second chakras meet—the front and back sacral chakras. Our sacral chakras regulate our personal emotional field and are often structurally compressed by our habitual thoughts. Our personal emotional field holds the light waves of the personal emotions we consciously and non-consciously feel about ourselves. They can be either flowing and energizing or congested and restricting.

Gently bring your awareness to the healthy container of love you created for yourself. Become curious about how your thoughts support your emotions in a healthy way. Invite your capacity for self love to expand.

Be open to fully receive the nourishing energy of the bio-plasma through your front and back sacral chakras. Align to the Win-Win Playground, in which you are fully worthy of nourishment, and open even more to receive. Feel the emotions that emerge in your awareness as your personal emotional field increases in flow. Your emotions can be a valuable fuel for positive change in your life.

Our personal energy field is a layered system of structural lines of light and fluid waves. The second, fourth and sixth chakras feed the emotional energies of self-love, compassion (love for others), and divine love, respectively. These fluid fields of love within us nourish the structural layer below.

The personal emotional field feeds and nourishes the structural etheric field beneath it. The etheric field is most influenced by physical impacts on the body, and, in turn, has the greatest influence on the physical body. If you stub your toe, for example, the etheric field can compress in that moment. Sending love into that area can help it decompress. This is one way to understand the healing power of touch. We are sending love into the etheric field, supporting expansion and flow within the structural lines of light, which then allows the physical body to function with greater vitality.

Next, move up the front of the spine to the joint between your lumbar and thoracic spine. This is the location of the 3rd chakra pair: the front and back solar plexus chakras. The solar plexus chakra is the primary regulator of our mental field.

The mental field is a structured field of yellow lines of light. Over time, when we engage in negative self talk in our minds or out loud, we create micro tears and compressions in our mental field that affect the flow of our emotional field which affects our etheric field and our body's vitality.

As we continue up the spine to the area behind the heart, we will find the fourth chakra—the heart chakra—which regulates the rose-colored astral field of compassionate love in our relationships. Within the framework of the Win-Win Playground, sending compassionate love out to others from the mindset of equality also supports the vitality of the structural mental field that sits within it.

Take a moment to tune into the fourth chakra and invite it to open fully to the matrix of equal love within the Win-Win Playground. Bathe yourself with the rose colored light of compassionate love as your heart chakra softens and opens. Visualize the rose light moving into your mental field, softening and vitalizing it, and then into your second chakra to support your growing capacity for expanded self-love. As you do this, gently rotate your hips to activate stuck emotional energy that is ready to release.

When this exercise feels complete, bring your awareness to the base of your neck where your front and back throat chakras reside. This is the fifth set of chakras in your chakra system, which regulates the spaciousness of the etheric template.

As you tune into the throat chakras and the spaciousness within your personal energy field, visualize the golden light of your core essence coming together with the spaciousness that results from "letting go of outcome." Our core essence and intentional body initiate our actions for positive change, while deep trust in the whole allows outcomes far greater than we can imagine to emerge.

Move up the chakra system by visualizing the center of your head behind the brows, where we find the sixth chakra pair—the front and back third-eye chakras. This chakra pair regulates the flowing field of divine love and grace within our personal energy field. The divine love within our personal energy field presents as opalescent rays of light.

Spend some time exploring your relationship to divine love. Soften any armor you may have due to religious or spiritual wounding and if it feels right to you, invite divine love and grace to increase your vitality. This is the highest and lightest frequency of love we resonate with in our fields. It is a part of us, and we have access to this light at all times.

As we open to receive divine love through all twelve of our chakras, we align with the field of miracles. I strongly feel that it is important to be open to these miracles happening in our lives without limiting. Limiting happens when we become too specific about what we want. For example, if you are house shopping, instead of thinking about physical attributes of a house, imagine the qualities your new home will give you—safety, laughter, space to share, cook and be with each other with ease. Try being open ended as you seek the things that nourish you and those around you. When we focus on increasing positive qualities of life, not specific physical things, we are opening to broader possibilities of nourishment within the Win-Win Playground.

Finally, bring your awareness to the top of your head to the seventh chakra—the crown chakra. This single chakra regulates the golden structural field of divine thought called the Ketheric Template.

This golden light permeates every cell of your body and extends outward to the edge of your personal energy field. The Ketheric Template is the field of divine thought—it is where the consciousness of your spiritual beliefs are held.

The more you align your intentions with the Win-Win Playground—recognizing yourself as an equal member of the whole, while honoring the unique expression of your core essence—the more coherent and resilient the boundary of your personal energy field becomes.

Your spiritual fields of divine will, love and thought work together to create your matrix system. This is why I talk about the importance of believing yourself equal to the whole to keep yourself in the Win-Win Playground. As soon as you drop into a predominate belief pattern of not being enough, or not worthy, your personal energy field constricts and the flow of energy into your field becomes restricted. You become walled off from the glory of life within you.

You are amazing.

You are life.

Life is amazing.

Breathe that in.

Relational Lineage and Energetic Extension

Alongside the energetic framework I describe here, I want to name an important relational lineage that has deeply informed my understanding of personal behavior and healing.

Terry Real, a relational therapist and teacher, offers a clear and compassionate model for understanding how couples move out of healthy connections and into maladaptive patterns. His work describes two primary relational axes. The first, how we position ourselves in comparison to others—one-up or one-down—and the second, how we lose connection—walled-off or boundaryless. These axes help us recognize how power, protection, and disconnection show up in our intimate relationships, families, and communities.

Real's model focuses on relational behavior—how we position ourselves in relation to others when we feel threatened, overwhelmed, or unsafe. When safe and calm, we can access our wise adult selves. We remain relational. We make decisions based on *us* rather than *me.*

For the most part, when we are tapped into our wise adult self and able to negotiate our needs with others effectively—while also listening and responding with love to their needs—we are playing in the Win-Win Playground.

However, if our habitual patterns of service-through-sacrifice, or cycles of depletion followed by resentment, begin shaping our perception of what we need, we quickly find ourselves in one of the maladaptive playgrounds. Our energy field cannot sustain unhealthy habits indefinitely—especially during seasons of illness, transition, or increased stress, when we are less resourced.

The work I offer in this book extends the relational awareness into the relationship between the personal energy field and the universal energy field.

The playground grid I present differs from the grid presented by Terry Real. In his model, he describes four maladaptive states—one-up and walled off, one-down and walled off, one-up and boundaryless, one-down and boundaryless.

In the model I offer, one quadrant represents equality and abundant connection with self and the whole—the Win-Win Playground. The Masochistic Playground corresponds to the one-down, walled off state. The Competitive Playground reflects the one-up, walled off state. The Human Grenade Playground represents a boundaryless energetic defense state that emerges when we become overwhelmed—whether positioned one-up or one-down in relation to others and the whole.

As you move through these pages, I invite you to consider how the maladaptive playground dynamics show up in your life. Notice not only how you respond on Terry Real's relational scale, but also what happens in your tissues, your breath, your posture, and your energetic boundaries as these patterns resonate.

From this perspective, relational dynamics are not only psychological or behavioral. They are also somatic and energetic experiences that shape our health, vitality, and sense of agency over time.

These models offer maps to help you become aware of your ever-changing patterns.

And as we move forward together in this exploration, it is important to note:

The map is not the territory.

How we act under stress is not the whole of who we are. It is not our deepest self—it is our protective patterns trying to help us survive.

I will now discuss the energetic habits that can bring you into the maladaptive playgrounds of the Masochistic Playground, the Competitive Playground and the Human Grenade Playground. With awareness, we regain choice, and we have the possibility to return once again, with love, to the Win-Win Playground.

The Masochist Playground: Forgetting Ourselves

We enter the Masochist Playground when we place ourselves "one-down"—when we believe that the highest good of others matters more than our own. In this state, we forget that we are equal members of the whole.

Here, love remains present—but it becomes distorted through over-endurance, suppression of needs, and a quiet belief that tending to ourselves is less important than tending to others. Understanding this playground through both a relational and energetic lens allows us to recognize it not as a flaw, but as a learned protection pattern—one that once kept us safe, and that can now be gently brought back into balance through awareness, compassion, and choice.

I notice this pattern in myself when I immediately jump up to help a member of my family—upon their request—without first pausing to check in with my body. Before I ask:

Do I actually have the capacity for this right now?

Before I feel into whether my *yes* is rooted in love-or in a survival habit.

There is great love in that impulse. And yet, there is also imbalance—between my love for my family and my love for myself. It may be subtle, but it is present.

When I act from that imbalance, I eventually notice a familiar depletion in my body. My chest tightens slightly. My throat constricts. My energy spoons drop. A faint irritation rises, followed by resentment.

Over time, I have come to recognize resentment as a messenger. It tells me I have stepped out of alignment with my highest good and into the Masochist Playground.

Now, that signal brings awareness.

It invites me to pause.

To step back into a container of love.

To take a breath—letting the exhale be slightly longer than the inhale.

I ask myself two questions.

Is this mine to do?

And is this mine to do now?

Sometimes the answer is still yes—but a cleaner yes. Sometimes it becomes a renegotiated yes. And sometimes it is a no.

In that pause, balance can be restored. My highest good can stand alongside the highest good of the person asking for help. And from that place, service becomes sustainable.

Before we move further, it is helpful to understand how this playground sustains itself. The Masochist pattern does not appear all at once. It forms through subtle habits of actions and beliefs that quietly reinforce one another over time. When we slow down and look closely, we can begin to see the two primary pathways that bring us into this one-down state—and keep us there.

Two Pathways into the Masochistic Playground

The two classic patterns that bring us into this playground are depleting actions and constricting beliefs.

Depleting Action

A common pattern among helpers, healers, and caregivers is the belief that service requires sacrifice. We might identify with the archetypes of the martyr, the savior, or the hero from a false belief that the love coming to us is based on our actions rather than as our right as an equal member of the whole.

When we attach to this belief, we create an energetic habit of depletion. We send more energy out than we allow to flow in. We override our own internal signals. We push through fatigue. We say yes when our body whispers no.

Over time, this imbalance erodes our vitality. We become tired, and ultimately, resentful.

Our field cannot sustain chronic one-way giving.

Constriction

The second pattern is constriction. We constrict the flow of love and grace when either we do not feel safe to receive or when we attach to the belief that we are not worthy of receiving.

Life can be hard. It can wear us down. When we make mistakes, instead of seeing them as valuable teachers—clarifying our "no" so we can stand more fully in our "yes"—we may attach to shame and tell ourselves:

If this is happening to me, I must deserve it. I must be bad.

Shame tightens the tissues. The diaphragm locks. The heart field narrows. The solar plexus chakra can become blocked or even move into reverse, sending bio-plasma out instead of receiving it. From this place of shame, we lose connection to our agency. We start to believe that we have to do things we don't want to do in order to get the things we want. The body learns to survive with diminished receiving.

Restoring Equal Flow

As you read these words, notice any constriction arising in your body.

Pause.

Tune into the field of God's love and grace that surrounds you. Take a few deep breaths, allowing the out-breath to be two seconds longer than the in-breath. With each breath, open yourself to receive.

Give yourself permission to feed yourself as an equal member of the whole. I recommend starting with the affirmation:

It is okay to receive more than I give.

This is not selfishness. This is recalibration. When your intention is to restore equal valuation with the whole, you are standing firmly in the Win-Win Playground. You are training yourself to hold bigger and bigger flows of energy, and with each training session, by keeping some of that energy for yourself, you become a brighter, more stable beacon of light on the planet.

When I practice this, I tune into my body and feel deeply into my tissues. I bring awareness to my heart and my core essence. From this internally connected place, I open to receive through the higher chakras and feel the golden light that enters from the higher realms. I envision the golden light dropping to the center of the

Earth. I feel love rising from the center of the Earth into my root chakra and back up to my heart as a soft warm red current. I allow the light to feed me. The two currents mix at the heart.

I experience God's grace entering my tissues as opalescent, multi-colored streams of light. I allow it to shift my cellular vibration, cell by cell. I allow it to soften my heart, restore compassion, and heal past woundings that once restricted love in my life. I reconnect more clearly with my core essence and I remember: I am enough. I am doing enough. I step back into the Win-Win Playground and co-create with God. I become the change I want to see in the world.

Barbara Brennan recommends taking one minute to fill your personal energy field with energy from the Universal Energy Field for each client or act of service. The simplest way to do this is through intention. You might say:

I am filling myself with the balanced energy of love from Heaven and Earth to meet all my needs and the needs of those around me for today.

You can do this at the beginning of the day or at any point when you notice depletion.

And yet, even with tools for restoring balance, many of us find ourselves returning to over-giving again and again. This is not because we lack discipline. It is often because something deeper is happening in the nervous system. There is a layer of this pattern that can feel surprisingly compelling—almost magnetic—and it deserves compassionate examination.

The Addictive Quality of Giving

There is another layer here that is harder to name.

Giving can be addictive.

When we give excessively, the body releases dopamine and oxytocin. We feel useful. Needed. Good. Superior to our own vulnerability. Over time, the nervous system can become dependent on that activation.

Helping becomes identity.

And if we stop helping, we may feel anxious. Who am I if I am not the strong one? The capable one? The generous one?

Addiction is not always about substances, sometimes it is about nervous system states.

Depleting generosity can become a self-soothing strategy.

From a nervous system perspective, giving temporarily reduces anxiety. When others are calm, approving, or appreciative, our bodies register relief. Stress hormones drop. Dopamine and oxytocin rise. We feel needed. We feel safe.

Over time, the body begins to associate over-giving with regulation. Generosity becomes less about love and more about preventing discomfort. We give to quiet tension. We give to avoid rejection. We give to stabilize the environment. The relief that follows reinforces the pattern. This is how depletion can take on an addictive quality. The short-term soothing masks the long-term cost.

For years, I did not recognize that my giving was also helping me feel safe. When I anticipated needs and met them before they were spoken, my body softened for a moment. I kept everyone happy, and carried more than my share. I felt useful, needed, and temporarily steady. What I did not see was the long arc forming underneath. Chronic depletion keeps the nervous system in subtle activation. Chronic activation alters immune signaling. Inflammation becomes one of the body's languages of imbalance.

When generosity becomes fused with identity and safety, depletion can accumulate quietly for years. The body will tolerate imbalance longer than we realize—until it cannot. What follows is not offered as a universal blueprint, but as one thread of my own lived experience, where chronic depletion eventually spoke through my immune system in a language I could no longer ignore.

Chronic Depletion as a Habit

Chronic depletion does not usually announce itself dramatically.

It builds quietly.

I learned this through my mother.

She was a devoted, loving woman. A "super mom." She gave tirelessly—to her children, her husband, her responsibilities. I internalized that model early: put others first, hold it all together, don't complain, keep going.

I carried that pattern into adulthood. I put my children first. I put my clients first. I managed the household so my husband could pour energy into his creative work. I told myself this was love.

And it was.

But it was also depletion.

Over time, my nervous system adapted to chronic overextension. I rarely paused to ask what I needed. I rarely received in proportion to what I gave. I overrode fatigue. I ignored subtle signals. I stayed in motion.

Chronic depletion stresses the nervous system. Chronic stress dysregulates immune signaling. Inflammation is one of the body's languages of imbalance.

In my forties, that language became unmistakable.

I developed Rheumatoid Arthritis so severe that my feet swelled to the point where I could not wear shoes.

At first, I experienced it as betrayal, then as unlucky genetics. But when I softened enough to listen, I began to see something else.

My arthritis was not a punishment. It was a messenger.

My immune system was doing what I had not done consciously: it was protesting the pattern of self-erasure in my life.

During my Advanced 2 CranioSacral Therapy training, I entered a period of deep personal process work. Some of the healing came quickly—what I call Fast Train moments. My Inner Wisdom told me clearly that I did not need to become Diplomat Certified in CranioSacral Therapy to do what I need to do in the world. In that moment I shifted out of the pattern of needing to associate with the highest accolades in my field to feel valuable and tuned inward to re-calibrate my self worth. There were profound attunements. I entered the black void of possibility and returned through the quantum field into cellular awareness, resonating with the deep purple frequency of self-worth. There were attunements to God's grace, to Archangels Michael, Gabriel, Raphael, and Uriel. There was a remembering that I was not alone inside my body.

But if I am honest, I do not believe the Fast Train moments alone healed my inflammation. The Slow Train did.

The Slow Train was:

Resting before exhaustion.

Saying no before resentment.

Receiving help without apology.

Allowing money to support me.

Sitting with the trees and remembering my roots.

Receiving and the Field of Oneness

For years, I have had a very top-heavy energy field—I have been very open through my higher chakras—but struggled receiving from the Earth.

Looking back, I found something curious.

As a child, I struggled with mild allergies. When tested, I discovered I was allergic to all grasses and nearly all trees. The exception? fruit trees. And the willow tree in our backyard.

At the time, it was simply a medical fact, nothing more.

Looking back, I noticed I was open to light descending from the heavens, yet less practiced at letting nourishment rise from the Earth. I welcomed inspiration, guidance, and divine knowing through my crown, yet struggled to root into the Earth and allow grounded nourishment to rise through my body. I reacted negatively to much of the natural world—except to the trees that nourish and bend.

The willow was my favorite place to play. I felt safe beneath it. The cherry tree beside it—still brings up fond memories.

I do not claim causation here. I simply hold curiosity.

I notice the symbolism.

I was comfortable receiving sweetness and softness. I was less comfortable receiving the raw grounding of the Earth.

When we chronically give from a spiritual belief system without receiving, we become energetically top-heavy. We draw from heaven but forget the importance of the roots. Our souls came to Earth at this time for a reason. They chose our ancestral lineages and cultural communities as the playground for our learning. It is up to us to find the safety in our environment that supports and nourishes us and to slow down enough so that we can be with the learning edge of our discomfort. Although it is not necessarily our job to heal every dysfunctional pattern each of our ancestors carried, we are the result of both the positive and negative aspects of everyone that came before us in our lineage. I invite you to spend time cultivating the positive, and when the negative comes up in your bodies, stay in a place of curiosity and wonder about what the learning this experience is bringing for you.

For me, healing required remembering my roots both physically and ancestrally.

I consciously began reconnecting to the trees. I would sit in the grass daily and place my hands on their bark and feel their steadiness. Trees do not apologize for receiving sunlight. They do not apologize for drawing nutrients from the soil. They stand in reciprocity. They are connected and supported by their neighbors through the fungal network system in the ground and work as a team. No tree stands alone.

During my daily meditations while sitting in the grass next to the mother tree in my local park, I opened to receiving. The trees showed me sacred geometry, helped me tune into my chakra system on a whole new level, and they showed me how to be in balance.

I began seeing golden light descending from above and warm, red Earth energy rising from below. I would let them meet at my heart. I would let my tissues soften. I would allow grace to enter not just my mind, but my cells.

Inflammation began to calm, not overnight, not dramatically, but steadily. Within six months, I no longer needed to take medication to decrease my inflammation. Within a year, I no longer had the blood markers for rheumatoid arthritis.

As my nervous system experienced safety—not from pushing myself into achieving external ideals of success but from receiving—my immune system slowly recalibrated. I will still occasionally have inflammation flare ups, and when these occur, I pause, go in and sit with my experience. I come from a long line of women with rheumatoid arthritis on my father's side. Sometimes I will feel a tension pattern arising in my body and when I ask: Is this mine to do? I get a "no". I pick up the tension pattern with love and return it to my ancestor, and say "I can't help you with this without harming myself". Other patterns are mine to shift. With these, I sit with the tension edge of what is emerging for me to learn. For others, simply connecting to my core essence is enough for those patterns to shift.

This is the Slow Train.

Healing from Rheumatoid Arthritis required more than technique. It required a shift in identity. I was not meant to be the source of everything. I was meant to be a conduit. When I softened my armor and opened to Plan B—to the spaciousness of Divine Will, and to divine love and grace moving through my life rather than my will gripping tightly—my body began to change.

This was not about perfection.

It was about participation in oneness.

The more I remembered my connection to trees, to angels, to the Earth beneath my feet, to the grace flowing from above—the more my body relaxed its defensive posture.

Inflammation softened.

Resentment softened.

Scarcity softened.

And slowly, steadily, I can stay longer in the Win-Win Playground—where I am nourished, and so are those around me—not because I sacrifice myself, but because I stand as an equal member of the whole.

***

When you notice yourself in the one-down playground and walled off due to feeling unworthy, return to receiving by saying again:

I am filling myself with the balanced energy of love from heaven and earth to support all my needs and the needs of those around me for today. I am an equal member of God's team.

Over time, this energetic process becomes a habit. Support becomes more automatic.

Receiving, I came to understand, is not just spiritual or relational. It extends into every domain where flow exists. This includes money. If we are uncomfortable receiving love, support, or rest, we are often uncomfortable receiving financial resources as well. The same energetic imbalance that fuels depletion in service can quietly shape our relationship with abundance.

The Masochist Playground and Money

For many who play in the Masochistic Playground, there is openness to the spiritual love coming through our higher chakras but imbalance in our connection and ability to receive through our root chakra from the Earth.

This imbalance can result in living in a matrix of financial scarcity. Money is energy—and many of us carry inherited fear and conditioning around it. As we expand our capacity to receive energy in general, knowing that keeping some for ourselves can be supporting ourselves and the whole equally, we increase the capacity of our healthy container around money.

Take a moment to notice how you respond to this statement:

It is okay to receive more money than I give.

If you habitually play in the Masochistic Playground, you will likely feel uncomfortable with this statement. Take a moment to breathe through the discomfort and notice any limiting beliefs that come up for you. A limiting belief, is any belief that causes a restriction pattern in your energetic field and/or tissues. Ask yourself, is this belief serving me? If it is causing a restriction pattern, then it isn't. Soften your gaze, deepen your breath and invite a more expansive belief to emerge from love.

Take a moment to write your new belief down.

***

Here is another statement to play with:

Money is energy, and energy is love.

Take a moment to check for body tension around this statement. Breathe, and invite softening as you come into loving neutrality with yourself in relationship to money.

***

Many people spend energetic resources trying to manifest a big financial windfall, without strengthening their energetic container to hold it. Without boundaries and receiving capacity, money leaks or destabilizes. This is especially true if we have non-conscious shame beliefs around having money. It is one reason many lottery winners are worse off financially years after winning the lottery then they were before.

One expansive view to contemplate, is that the energetic container that flexibly holds and manages the flow of money can be used to fully support experiences of wonder, creativity and bliss in our lives. Consider the Slow Train here. What subtle but profound changes can you make to be in healthier relationship to the flow of money?

The typical Masochist Playground response is: *I don't need money to be happy*—and yes—that is partially true. Money does not create happiness, but when basic needs are met—nourishing food, supportive shelter, and the most precious resource—time to engage in our creative projects is available—ease of access to our wise, happy adult-self increases.

If it feels right to you, consciously expand your capacity to be in the healthy flow of money. Not to hoard. Not from fear. But from love.

Feel the energy of the Earth entering your root chakra and filling your field with grounded, compassionate love. If you tend to play in the depleting or constricting patterns of the Masochist Playground, this practice will increase your capacity to receive nurturance, hold a larger container of energy in your personal field and over time, will bring our field into balanced receiving of the energies of Heaven and Earth.

As your container strengthens and expands in a healthy way, notice how you are inspired to use money in ways that support positive change in both yourself and the whole.

Stay playful. Stay patient. Generational patterns and non-conscious beliefs are complex. Healing unfolds in layers. Invite your highest self to come on board to bring you the external resources and show you the internal changes needed to be made for your highest good when the time is right.

Stay compassionate with yourself, and look for those subtle but profound changes that support stepping more deeply into the Win-Win Playground where all your needs and the needs of those around you are fully met.

If you tend to play in the Competitive Playground, you are likely openly receiving money, but need to move more into your heart and increase compassionate flow outwards. Connecting to your heart chakra, will help you see more clearly where you are out of balance and the direction of the outward flow that is right for you.

Reflective Pause: Money and Safety

Pause for a moment.

Notice your breath.

Let your exhale be slightly longer than your inhale.

Now gently say, either out loud or internally:

It is safe for me to receive.

It is safe for me to have enough.

It is safe for me to express my needs.

It is safe for my needs to be fully met.

Notice what happens in your body.

Does your chest tighten?

Does your jaw clench?

Does your belly harden?

There is no right answer.

Simply notice.

Your body's response is information, not judgment.

If you feel tension arise, you might choose to work gently with it using a clearing practice. One practice I return to often is envisioning myself in a safe circle of love. I breathe in that love until my tissues soften. This allows restriction patterns to loosen before they harden into resentment or contraction.

If you sense that more support is needed, you may wish to turn to Habit #3: *Be the Light*, and experiment with the Ho'oponopono practice for deeper integration.

Masochistic Survival Trait: People Pleasing

While over-giving becomes an identity pattern reinforced by self-worth attached to a role and the subtle dopamine reward of creating happiness in your environment, people-pleasing arises more directly from a survival response in the nervous system. From a nervous system perspective, this is known as "fawning"—a social survival response of the sympathetic nervous system.

What happens is that when in a stressful situation, the social vagal nervous system engages to defuse perceived stress in others by becoming overly pleasant and accommodating. We place other's needs above our own, not from a sense of being unworthy, but from a sense of feeling unsafe. We fear that if we stand up for ourselves, and express our needs, we will be rejected or even harmed. We make ourselves purposefully small and energetically invisible unless we are showing others what a great job we can do by putting their needs before our own. This pattern is often non-conscious.

This energetic pattern of fawning can start as early as in utero, but typically starts before the age of 4 years old. During this stage of development, we have no agency. We cannot say "no" and step out of an unhealthy playground dynamic. We do what we can to protect ourselves within our family. We learn to fawn to decrease the stress within the home. When we become aware of this pattern in our lives, we regain choice.

As fawning comes into awareness, we often notice signs of stress in the body—especially shallow breathing. Breath is a bridge back to now. Allowing the out-breath to be two seconds longer than the in-breath brings us out of the time capsule of early wounding and back into present-time flow.

When you notice yourself in the one-down playground and walled off due to feeling unsafe, return to receiving by saying again:

Right now, in this present moment, I am safe and surrounded by God's love and grace. I open to fully receive that love and grace in my life. I am an equal member of God's team, and God is supporting me to do our work fully.

Whether the pattern expresses as over-giving, scarcity, inflammation, or people-pleasing, the invitation is the same. We are being asked to remember our equal place in the whole. We are being invited to move from survival into conscious participation. The shift does not require force. It requires awareness, breath, and a willingness to receive as much as we give.

The Gifts Hidden Within the Masochistic Pattern

It is important to name something clearly here.

The Masochist Playground is not born from lack of love, but rather from an abundance of it.

Many who play in this playground have enormous outward heart flow. We are attuned, responsive, devoted, and capable of deep compassion. We feel others' needs quickly. We sense subtle shifts in the field. We are often spiritually open, receptive through the crown, and connected to guidance beyond our own thinking mind. These are not weaknesses; they are gifts.

The imbalance arises when outward flow is not matched by grounded receiving, and when we accept the flow of grace into our upper chakras but we do not allow nourishment of grace to rise from below. In these situations we are blending with the hierarchial structure of the competitive playground; we are placing giving over receiving and spiritual grace over physical grace. I highly recommend touching the ground daily with your feet, and if you work regularly with a computer, use a grounding mat. Self care is not optional for those who have habitually lived in the Masochist Playground.

In my own case, one of my teachers told me I had one of the largest outward heart flows she had ever seen. That capacity did not need to be reduced. It needed to be rooted. I needed to learn that it is safe to receive, and I am on that journey.

The Win-Win Playground does not ask us to shrink our gifts.

It asks us to balance them.

When strong outward flow is paired with grounded receiving and inward holding, the same sensitivity that once led to depletion becomes sustainable leadership. The same compassion that once created exhaustion becomes regenerative service.

The gifts are not the problem, it is imbalance that creates the depletion pattern found in the Masochist Playground.

When we honor the gifts within the Masochistic pattern while strengthening our capacity to receive, something shifts. The outward flow of love remains — but it becomes rooted, sustainable, and mutually nourishing. This is the doorway back to the Win-Win Playground.

Shifting from the Masochistic to the Win-Win Playground

When we commit to choosing the Win-Win Playground, we begin building a simple but powerful habit: we check in before saying yes. We remember that we are allowed to change our minds if an action moves us into depletion. We remember that sustainable service requires equal nourishment between ourselves and others.

We continue to practice holding a healthy container of love for ourselves, and fill the container each day with enough love that we still have some for ourselves at the end of the day.

***

If you notice yourself slipping into Masochist energy, gently re-align.

Soften your gaze.

Take a breath.

Return to the balanced current of Heaven and Earth meeting in your heart.

Open to what is best for you and for the whole equally.

You are not meant to be the source.

You are meant to be a conduit.

The gifts of the Masochistic pattern — empathy, guidance, heart-centered generosity — are not flaws. They are strengths waiting for roots.

When outward love is paired with inward receiving, your field stabilizes.

Service becomes sustainable.

Money becomes nourishing.

Inflammation softens.

Resentment dissolves before it hardens.

You are not here to disappear.

You are here to participate.

Stand as an equal member of the whole.

And from that grounded, rooted, nourished place —step again into the Win-Win Playground.

If you find yourself in a people-pleasing pattern—pause and breathe yourself back into the safety of now. Then say:

I am an equal member of God's team. I am safe. My needs are equally important to the needs of the whole.

Notice what shifts in your body when you speak that truth.

There is a lot of discussion about the stress patterns of the sympathetic nervous system—fight, flight and fawn. What is less often talked about is that when regulated, it is also the source of wonder, inspiration and blissed-in experiences. Likewise, our parasympathetic nervous system under stress shows up as flaccidity in the tissues or the freeze response. The parasympathetic nervous system when regulated presents itsself as the capacity to rest, relax, reset and recharge. It helps us to connect authentically to our whole selves and to be present enough to indulge in the pauses in our lives. It is in these pauses that the true change in our nervous systems happen and the new way forward has the space to creatively emerge into our conscious awareness.

We energetically feed that on which we focus.

When we focus exclusively on stress, we reinforce stressful patterns in our lives. When we choose to focus on wonder and inspiration, we begin feeding those neural pathways instead. As you tune into your sympathetic nervous system, ask gently:

What's missing?

Take time to open yourself to increasing wonder, creativity and embodied bliss in your life. Look around for what inspires you. Feed those energies with your attention and see what evolves.

Step back onto the Win-Win Playground. As you go about your day, you can say silently to yourself:

I am the child of abundant and loving Parents.

God wants you to thrive. The consciousness of the Earth wants you to thrive. Let every molecule of your body attune to abundance and grace. Open all of your chakras equally to receive. Follow your bliss.

As we soften our armor and invite the spaciousness of Divine Will to expand our fields, we expand our capacity as vessels of love and grace and our bodies begin to change. Not because we sacrifice ourselves, but because we stand as equal members of the whole.

In this playground of life, our personal energy field is constantly shifting as we soften armor and become clearer beacons of light. At the same time, our soul collaborates with the Divine to create learning environments that are "just right" for our unique evolution.

As awareness grows, we step out of victimhood and into conscious choice. We start to co-create our learning experiences.

We choose love.

We choose service that nourishes.

We choose creative expansion.

We choose—again and again—the Win-Win Playground.

The Competitive Playground: "One-Up" and "Walled Off"

The energetic pattern of the Competitive Playground is this: we open to nourishment and flow for ourselves at the expense of the whole.

We enter the Competitive Playground when the focus of our personal energy field shifts from the heart to the head or from the heart to the pelvis. These shifts away from heart centered being often stem from our habitual thinking about ourselves in relation to the whole. Many of these beliefs developed in response to our childhood wounding experiences. The overwhelm from our early wounding creates a subtle separation from the Universal Energy Field. In the Competitive Playground, we shift from "Let *Thy* will be done" to "Let *My* will be done". The back chakras enlarge pushing the intentional line forward, and overtime energetic armoring around the heart restricts both the front and back heart chakra; walling you off from compassionate connection to others. The armor can cause a depleting pattern overtime, especially when you find yourself in a role of being in service due to a sense of duty or the belief that it is your role to decrease the suffering of others.

When Intellect Rules

When our energy moves from our heart to our head, we move away from the present, compassionate, whole-brain connection of the Win-Win Playground and become left-brain dominant. As this happens, we lose access to the bigger picture and may begin micro-managing our own lives—and the lives of those around us—from a one-up position. We also move from compassionate presence to worrying about the future.

My children are now adults—twenty-three and twenty years old—but as most parents know, that doesn't mean they are always able to make Win-Win decisions.

When I am grounded and present, I know that the decisions they are making for their lives are theirs to make. And yet, when my children begin to struggle and come to me for advice, I notice a familiar tendency to go far beyond what they are actually asking.

I might spend hours job-searching for my son, or researching graduate programs and housing options for my oldest. My impulse is to provide them with a five-year plan for their lives—when what they are really asking for is a sounding board, a place to think out loud so they can discover what is right for themselves.

When I go down this planning rabbit hole, I feel a rush of excitement—like there's a grand puzzle to solve, and I'm the one who can solve it best! There's a thrill in the challenge. My heart races a little—almost like caffeine in my chest. And at the same time, I notice something else. My heart feels slightly less open. I've lost connection to the equality of the whole.

I forget that my children also have a higher self—guiding their decision-making, including the timing of their mistakes and their successes, all as part of their own soul's journey. I move one-up and forget to notice the core-essence in my children—that beautiful spark of gold light that exists in every cell of their body.

Over time, I learned to pause and ask a simple question: "Do you want ideas, or do you just want me to listen?"

When I do this, I stay in present connection with my children. Their bodies soften. So does mine.

They have given me feedback. They have told me they like—and want—to be friends with the person I am becoming. That tiny pivot is the difference between "one-up" and Win-Win.

***

Take a moment to think of a time when you dropped into planning mode because you felt like you could solve someone else's problems better than them. Notice: where you feel tension in your body—and does it come with openness, or with subtle closing of the heart? Notice the subtle separation that has occurred as well as the hoarding of energy from the whole when we start planning from a place of worry.

Take a moment now to invite your energy system to re-center around your heart chakra. Visualize the person you put one down through the golden light of their core essence. You can use your imagination to picture them with a golden glow. Allow the golden glow to expand to every cell of their body. This practice helps to reset your trust in each person as equal members of the whole.

When left-brain dominance becomes habitual, we begin to see the world through a lens of judgment. This is the Competitive Playground, where our internal voice critiques others. This action is motivated by the insecurity felt by our wounded child-self. We forget that we are all equally children of God—and that each of us has a "Higher Self" working with Divine timing to guide loving change in our lives.

In both the Masochist Playground and the Competitive Playground, we look inward through judgement. When we judge ourselves "one down," we restrict the nourishing flow of God's love and grace and step into the Masochist Playground. When we judge ourselves "one up," we may still feel nourished and energized—but we become walled off from awareness of the beauty of God's energy moving through others and step into the Competitive Playground. In Real's model, we become "one-up" and "walled off."

In the Competitive Playground, we drift away from kindness and compassion and begin playing with the energies of comparison, certainty, and competitiveness. Our heart chakra compresses or even closes and we can begin to hoard energy for our personal agendas.

Energetically, this creates imbalance. The personal energy field becomes expanded around the head and constricted around the heart and feet. We clearly see this pattern in behaviors such as religious fanaticism, judgment-driven political analysis, guru culture, and rigid scientific materialism—anywhere certainty replaces curiosity and external authority replaces the deep connection to self.

Labeling

On a more subtle level, this playground shows up as labeling others, pushing a personal agenda without regard for the needs of the whole, and attaching to hierarchical systems.

At its core, the Competitive Playground emerges when insecurity drives us to take energy, recognition, or resources without regard for the consequences those actions have on those around us.

When we label others—placing them in a box and deciding who they are—we create an energetic fixation. We move out of loving alignment and into a one-up position that diminishes our ability to perceive the beautiful, complex, multidimensional light in each of us. When our convictions are strong and reinforced by those around us, the people receiving those labels may begin to doubt their own inner light.

We may feel nourished by our certainty, while others quietly suffer.

My colleague Chas Perry, PhD, has noted that the word *invalid* comes from the Latin word *invalidare* meaning "to weaken, to make ineffective". Our convictions, when forceful, can invalidate those around us. Even when we believe we are "helping," when we do onto others, the energetic impact can be harmful. As we attach to our perception of what is right, we invalidate the experience of those around us, negating their version of reality, feelings, and sense of what is right for them.

Competitive dynamics also show up personally when our actions and agendas are fueled by insecurity rather than love. We move into the mindset, "May *my* will be done", and start pushing a personal agenda. We take more than our share of resources. We lose connection to the whole and become imbalanced participants in society. When we push our own agenda from an isolated place, others suffer.

I recognized this pattern in myself during advanced personal process work. At the time, I was on track to obtain Diplomat Certification in CranioSacral Therapy. This is the highest certification one can receive in this field. When I tuned into the energy fueling that decision, I was guided to let it go. The certification would have benefited me personally—more letters after my name—but it did not feel aligned with the highest good of the whole.

Even now, when I test for alignment using the statement:

Engaging in the Diplomat Certification process is for my highest good and the highest good of the whole,

I receive a clear "yes" for myself—and a clear "no" for the whole. The answer is unmistakable: it is not a Win-Win choice.

Yes, I would gain knowledge and experience. And I also ask: What resources would this take away from the whole that could be better used elsewhere?

Competitive environments often foster hierarchical dynamics—structures where power, status or worth are ranked rather than shared. When "winning" becomes more important than integrity: harm follows. Some corporate, academic, and political systems intentionally reinforce this pattern.

If you find yourself in such an environment, trust that a better path exists. Leaving—at the right time—can be an act of re-alignment, not failure. God always has a Plan B, and it is often far more wondrous and nourishing than anything we can imagine in the moment.

When Passion Rules

Another "one up" and "walled off" pattern we encounter in the Competitive Playground arises when our energy shifts from the heart down into the pelvis. In this state, passion and drive fuel our projects and ambitions—but without sufficient regard for the impact our hyper-focused intensity may be having on those around us. Many brilliant thinkers, innovators, and project leaders fall into this pattern.

I chose to marry a genius. My business partner is also a genius. As a result, both my personal and professional lives have been shaped by the gifts—and the challenges—of this dynamic.

My husband likely has an IQ in the 160–170 range and earned his PhD in pure mathematics from UC Berkeley. The word I would most readily use to describe him in our relationship is *kind*—until he becomes deeply absorbed in a project. When that happens, he can grow distant and hyper-focused. He forgets to eat, loses track of time, and becomes agitated when things are not unfolding the way he expects. Sound familiar?

My husband is very aware that when he enters this state, he can become selfish with time. He may work late into the night and unintentionally forget family responsibilities—classic Competitive Playground dynamics.

Because we have made a conscious commitment to kindness in our relationship, and with the support of Terry Real's *The New Rules of Marriage*, I have learned to shift from complaint to request. Rather than criticizing, I name what I need from my wise adult self.

In response, my husband has been actively working on accountability. When he commits to something, he now offers a realistic timeframe, and with occasional reminders, he is increasingly successful at following through and being accountable. This is what returning to the Win-Win Playground looks like in practice: not perfection, but awareness, responsibility, and repair.

If you notice yourself becoming so absorbed in a project or passion that you lose connection with the people around you, pause. Take a breath. Gently bring your energy back into your heart.

Consider saying:

I am co-creating this project with Love. I feel Love's support. Love is the energy that brings positive change.

From the heart, passion becomes creative rather than consuming—and our work nourishes rather than depletes the relationships that matter most.

The Origins of the Competitive Patterning

As children, we begin to armor our hearts when we feel betrayed by a significant caregiver. This is often, but not always, the caregiver of the opposite sex to you. We learn to do things by ourselves. To rely on our own skills and to build the skills we need to be successful in the world so we don't have to rely on others. As our skills build, we can start to develop a hero complex or God complex, trying to prevent others from feeling the wounds we felt as children- often successfully to some extent. Due to the walled off nature of this pattern, we often create deep energetic depletion patterns as we tell ourselves stories such as:

"I am trying to get everything done, and I feel like I'm only getting everything half way done."

"I receive so I can give out ten fold."

Each of these statements show a depletion pattern that stems from a walled off pattern from the Universal Energy Field. We place ourselves one-up from others and source energy, feeling like we have a mission to give, serve, and that doing so in a big way makes us special, needed. We start telling ourselves the story that our value stems from what we do, not simply from who we are.

Pause to Return to the Win-Win

Take a moment to soften your gaze.

Notice where your energy is right now.

Is it gathered in your head?

In your pelvis?

Or resting gently in your heart?

***

Bring one hand to your chest and take a slow breath in through your nose. Let your exhale be just a little longer than your inhale.

If there is a project, passion, or responsibility currently holding your attention, gently ask yourself:

- *Am I creating from connection—or from urgency?*

- *Who around me might need my presence right now?*

- *What would it feel like to bring this work back into my heart?*

There is nothing to fix.

Only an invitation to return.

When you are ready, silently affirm:

I choose to co-create from love. My passion is supported by grace. I can act on what I love with full connection to the equal playing field.

Stay here for one or two more breaths. Then continue reading when your body feels settled.

The Gifts Hidden in the Competitive Pattern

Every maladaptive playground contains a seed of brilliance.

The Competitive Playground does not emerge because we are flawed. It emerges because we are gifted.

When energy gathers in the head, there is intelligence.

There is vision.

There is strategic capacity.

There is the ability to see systems and anticipate outcomes.

When energy gathers in the pelvis, there is passion.

There is drive.

There is the courage to initiate.

There is life force willing to move mountains.

The Competitive pattern often arises in those who are capable. In those who can lead. In those who feel the call to create something meaningful in the world.

The problem is not the brilliance. The problem is the disconnection from the heart.

Left-brain precision becomes micromanagement when unbalanced. Drive becomes domination when untethered from compassion. Vision becomes hierarchy when disconnected from equality.

But when brought back into the heart, these same qualities become extraordinary gifts.

Intellect becomes discernment.

Passion becomes creative devotion.

Leadership becomes stewardship.

Ambition becomes sacred service.

Some of the most powerful positive change makers in history have strong Competitive energy — but it is regulated by humility, curiosity, and love.

The goal is not to eliminate your drive.

The goal is to root it in the Win-Win Playground.

If you recognize yourself in the Competitive pattern, take a breath.

You likely carry tremendous capacity.

The invitation is not to shrink.

It is to soften.

Bring your brilliance back into your heart.

And let it serve what you love and the whole equally.

Collective One-Up Dynamics: When Individual Certainty Scales into Harm

When we explore the Competitive Playground at the individual level, we see a familiar pattern: a shift into certainty, comparison, and control. We become "one up," believing we know more, see more clearly, or are acting more rightly than others. This stance often emerges not from malice, but from insecurity and fear. It offers temporary relief by restoring a sense of order and control.

What is less obvious—and far more impactful—is what happens when this individual pattern scales to the collective.

From Individual Protection to Collective Identity

Human nervous systems are social. When we feel threatened, we instinctively look for others who share our perspective. Belonging regulates fear. Agreement soothes uncertainty. Over time, individual "one-up" positions can harden into group identity.

This is the moment when the Competitive Playground expands from the *me versus you* into the *us versus them* dynamic.

At this stage, collective one-up dynamics begin to take shape. Groups form around shared beliefs, shared fears, and shared stories about what is right, dangerous, or unacceptable. The group offers a sense of safety—but at a cost. Curiosity narrows. Complexity flattens. Nuances become difficult to hold.

The question quietly shifts from:

"What is true?" to *"Who is right?"*

Collective one-up situations can happen in large groups—as well as in small families.

A few years ago, I worked with a seventy-year-old electrical engineer who had a strong and clear sense of what was right for his own body.

In response to the stress of the COVID pandemic, some members of his family became very certain about what they believed was the right way forward for everyone. Despite my client's careful inner check-in—and his knowing that receiving one vaccine, but not two, felt aligned for him—he was repeatedly pressured by his children to receive the second dose.

Eventually, not because his inner knowing had changed, but because he wanted to preserve peace and connection, he agreed.

In that moment, belonging became conditional.

This is how collective one-up dynamics often scale—not through explosions or overt cruelty, but through a quiet narrowing of who is allowed to have agency in their experience.

The Chemistry of Certainty

Collective one-up dynamics are reinforced not only socially, but biologically.

When we feel superior or aligned with a group that shares our views, the brain releases oxytocin—the same hormone associated with bonding and trust. When that bonding is paired with judgment or shared outrage, the chemistry can become addictive. Complaining together, labeling others, and reinforcing group identity can feel euphoric in the short term.

This is not a moral failure. It is a nervous-system response.

The problem arises when this temporary regulation becomes a long-term strategy.

How Collective One-Up Reduces Choice

As collective certainty strengthens, several things begin to happen:

- Curiosity declines.

- Listening becomes selective.

- Dissent feels threatening.

- Complexity is experienced as destabilizing.

From within a collective one-up position, it becomes increasingly difficult to stay connected to the humanity of those outside the group. We may still believe we are acting from love—but love becomes conditional, armored, and selective.

We've seen this clearly in recent increasing political polarization in the United States, where members of each of the major parties have engaged in name calling, negative stereotyping and acceptance of strategies designed to win at any cost rather than serving the whole.

At this stage, harm does not usually appear dramatic. It appears justified.

We tell ourselves:

- "This is necessary."

- "They brought this on themselves."

- "There is no other option."

Choice narrows—not because alternatives do not exist, but because we can no longer see them.

The Bridge to the Human Grenade Playground

Collective one-up dynamics is one of the primary **on-ramps** to the Human Grenade Playground.

When certainty hardens into dehumanization, when fear overrides compassion, and when belonging requires someone else to be cast "one down," the system becomes unstable. Boundaryless actions begin to feel acceptable. Shame, denial, and hopelessness emerge—either directed outward or inward.

It is important to pause here.

Most people who enter the Human Grenade Playground do not begin there. They arrive through gradual escalation—often believing they are protecting what matters most.

Understanding this progression matters, because it restores humility and choice.

A Moment of Reflection

Take a breath.

As you read these words, notice what happens in your body when you think about groups you belong to—political, professional, spiritual, or cultural.

- Do you feel warmth or coldness in some part of your body?

- Is there tightness present?

- Do you have a strong sense of certainty about your group identity, with the sense that those not in your group are less than you in some way?

- Is there defensiveness that arises if someone questions your group or becomes curious about you?

There is no right or wrong response.

Simply notice.

Collective one-up dynamics are not a sign that something has gone terribly wrong. They are a sign that fear is asking for reassurance, and that reassurance has been outsourced to connection based on fear and separation rather than love and synergy.

The Human Grenade Playground: Deep Disconnection

We step into the Human Grenade Playground when our personal energy field—and thus our actions—become boundaryless. This emerges when separation from love becomes extreme and the nervous system locks into survival-based roles: victim, persecutor, and rescuer. We begin to label each other in these roles, and lose perspective of each other's humanity in a boundaryless way. In this state, our actions cause harm to ourselves and others, while we sincerely believe these actions are justified.

This playground is not entered because someone is "bad." It emerges when fear overwhelms our capacity for loving connection.

When you notice this pattern—either in yourself or around you—pause.

Take a breath.

Soften your armor.

Bring awareness back to your heart.

Reconnect with Grace.

When Fear Mixes with Love

Many of the most painful moments in our lives happen when fear mixes with love. We act from a sincere desire to protect ourselves or others, without the regulating presence of compassion and humility.

In these moments:

- Certainty replaces curiosity.

- Protection overrides discernment.

- Ends begin to justify means.

The Human Grenade Playground is entered not because love disappears, but because love becomes armored.

When you notice fear driving your decisions, pause. Ask yourself gently: "What am I trying to protect right now?"

Sometimes protection is appropriate. But when protection becomes a long-held habit, it creates energetic fixations that restrict the flow of Love and Freedom—both within and between us. Walled-off patterns are seen in the Masochist and Competitive Playgrounds, and the boundaryless patterns are seen in The Human Grenade Playground.

I've caught myself on this edge of overwhelm, when my masochistic depletion pattern turns boundaryless and I start getting hysterical—sending out spiked energy to those around me in an unconscious attempt to push my family away.

In the past, this pattern was larger and more damaging. At my worst, I would become mean and send out verbal barbs along with the energetic spikes of hysteria.

Now, I can sometimes feel the exact moment my field goes boundaryless—my breath shortens, and urgency spikes outward. When I notice that, I stop.

I say, "I'm overwhelmed. I need ten minutes."

I walk. I breathe. And I return when my heart is back online.

I repair faster—not because I'm better, but because awareness gives me a doorway out.

Barbara Brennan described twelve Energetic Defense Systems in her book *Hands of Light: A Guide to Healing Through the Human Energy Field.* I am including my current understanding of the seven patterns that have the strongest boundaryless energetic qualities below. These patterns are not who we are. They are who we are not. They are the patterns that emerge when we step out of connection to our core essence and into an early childhood protection pattern. As you read through each boundaryless protection pattern, notice if familiar physical tension patterns emerge in your awareness.

Take breaks if needed, or skip this section and come back to it slowly. Keep returning to breath, and invite the consciousness of your younger patterns to come into the now. Reconnect them to the part of you that is your wise adult self—the part of you that is present, capable and that has the discernment and the power to keep yourself safe.

As you read this section, you may start recognizing these patterns in your family and co-workers. I encourage you to let that go for now. It is easier to see patterns in others than feel them within ourselves. Let's stay with our own personal process here.

We are going to do this within a container of love. Take a moment to feel yourself in a bubble of love, fully supported and nourished. Breathe in that love and let it support you as you notice the physical and energetic patterns within you that come up under stress. We are inviting these patterns to come up lightly—just enough to build a bridge of awareness between your mind and body—so each pattern can release with ease, returning you to the present as it softens.

If this level of detail feels like too much today, you can skip ahead to "The Cost of One-Up Certainty" and return later.

Verbal Denial is when you create a false reality that feels safe to you, choosing conviction over curiosity. You lose the big picture. There is often an energetic block in the neck that separates the mind from the body, along with difficulty feeling grounded. There is deep separation from the nourishing field of Love and Freedom. Verbal denial can be internal dialogue with oneself that goes one-up "only I am capable of doing this" or one-down "I am only loveable if I act this way". It becomes boundaryless when you try to convince others of your narrow perspective in an effort to feel your own aliveness.

The Hook occurs when you disconnect from your agency as the creator of your life and consciously or unconsciously label yourself as the victim, and others as the persecutor or the rescuer. This pattern can be obvious or subtle and typically occurs when we perceive we are being threatened by an individual or group. It can also occur when we transfer our agency over our healing journey to the health care professionals around us. The hook often comes from the top of our head, drawing energy up and out and creating a depletion pattern in the body, which makes it difficult to receive nourishing love energy from the Earth through grounding.

The Mental Grasp pattern is also focused around the head and occurs when you won't let go of someone's field until you are certain that they agree with your "right" decision. It is a pattern of connecting through negative excitement and certainty rather than compassion and curiosity.

Tentacles is a complicated protection pattern. It is linked to deep feelings of shame and hopelessness and stems from a distorted view of your core essence. You don't see your golden shadow—your beauty, agency, creative capacity and value. You deeply struggle with humiliation and feel strongly "one-down." You become boundaryless when you attempt to control the behavior of those around you through passive-aggressiveness actions, such as silent brooding used as punishment. You complain rather than request because making requests feels humiliating. What is often most helpful here is finding a healthy release for anger, learning to give in ways that feel right, and then—over time—opening to the pleasure that comes with reconnecting to your agency.

Verbal Arrows can show up through name-calling and complaining. We do this as a protection pattern when we want to shift the focus from ourselves to others. We can also shoot verbal arrows if we do not have healthy ways of releasing anger. We may shoot an arrow at a loved one, hoping it will be painful enough to elicit anger in them—allowing us to release our own anger in a way that humiliates the other and avoids our own sense of embarrassment.

Hysteria is the absence of emotional boundary containment. Someone in this pattern may respond to a verbal arrow by allowing their energy field to explode—shooting arrows at everyone in a room. The protection purpose of this pattern can be to clear the room by creating powerful energetic chaos. It can be fueled by the childhood belief that "If I am overwhelmed, I can make everyone around me overwhelmed too, then I will be left alone." If you grew up in a household in which creating energetic chaos was a way to form connection, what one might describe as a trauma bond, your inner child, in times of stress may create this pattern in an effort to reach out for help and connection when stressed.

Power-Will Display is when you use a powerful display of your will to compel others to join your agenda. You expand and brighten your aura to such a degree that there is no question of who is in charge. From a protection standpoint, your bright aura says: "Don't mess with me!" From a connection standpoint your aura is trying to create followers to from a place of power- over others rather than acknowledging each individuals internal power and connection to core essence.

If you recognized yourself in any of these protection patterns, pause here and offer yourself kindness.

Awareness is the beginning of repair.

Our habitual protection patterns typically develop in our first four to eight years of life, when we did not have agency over our lives. As we age and become under stress, we often fall back into these early protection patterns.

Awareness restores choice.

As we become aware that we have moved into a habitual protection pattern, we can ask: "Is this pattern still serving me?"

The answer is often "no," and sometimes "partially"

When we move into a younger protection pattern, there is a part of our tissue consciousness that is stuck at the age the pattern developed. We can connect to that part with loving kindness and ask it if it has any unfulfilled needs. We can then choose to re-parent that part of ourselves whose needs were not met by allowing our wise adult self to be in loving presence with our younger self—and then inviting that younger self into current time.

Over time, our awareness of these patterns—and the speed of our recovery—improves, restoring choice and supporting us to step back into authentic relationship with our wise adult self and the Win-Win Playground.

The Cost of Boundaryless "One-Up" Certainty

A common Human Grenade dynamic arises when we move into the "one-up" and "boundaryless" position of acting from the belief we know what is right for others without being invited into their process.

This often shows up as:

- Offering unsolicited advice

- Labeling or categorizing others

- Acting "for someone's own good" without consent

Even when well-intentioned, these actions can undermine autonomy and deepen separation.

Please take this gently but clearly: unsolicited advice often comes from separation.

It is important to remember that "one up" can feel very good in the body. There is often a surge of endorphins and oxytocin—the brain's feel-good chemistry—which can reinforce a distorted sense of righteousness. From inside this state, our unsolicited advice can feel justified.

When we are truly aligned with the Win-Win Playground, we trust the timing of another person's journey inward towards their authentic, wise adult, self. We offer presence instead of control. We ask before acting. We stay curious. We understand that our perception of their experience creates a story in our minds about that experience, but it is not their experience.

For each of us, the timing of unconscious patterns coming into conscious awareness is guided by right timing that is being con-trolled by our Higher-Self—the part of us that is whole, healthy, and knows the best way forward for growth. To support each other, look for the core essence of those around you that are ac-tivating you. Any time you find yourself labeling or categorizing someone, you are being activated by some aspect of them for your own growth.

When you start seeing others from a lens of past trauma, shift your perspective to the complex, flawed embodiment of love that each of us are. Try to see their light. Stay curious about their process. You may be surprised at what you learn.

Parents of young children act on their behalf by creating routines and making decisions for the family. As these children become teenagers, parents move through the process of letting go of that decision making. As children age, they become better and better at tuning in and making the right decisions for themselves as they develop their wise adult selves. This process happens over years and is fraught with issues of control on both sides. Both parents and children will make mistakes, and if lucky, they into develop wise-adult to wise-adult relationships in the end.

When our adult children or other family members are ill, incapacitated in some way, struggle with addiction issues or mental health issues, this process becomes even more complicated. The right way forward in these situations is never simple and we often find ourselves swinging between the four playgrounds as we navigate our fears, love, connection and disconnection.

As you get activated by those you love, notice your tissue responses, the effects on your breath, and be compassionate with yourself. I will be introducing a tool for shifting ourselves out of activation in Habit #3: Be the Light. If you have a loved one, who is staunchly having fun in the Human Grenade playground, check in to what the right Win-Win option is for you. No one can make the decision about whether you should stay engaged or not, or how to stay engaged without harming yourself. The answers will come not from checking out, but rather by checking in with your higher-self.

If you ever hear "You should…", it can be a sign that the speaker (you or someone speaking to you) has slipped into a one-up, and boundaryless Human Grenade dynamic.

I encourage you to set the intention "I will not "should" on myself or others." Yes, this phrase will likely bring up another sh__ word into your awareness. It is on purpose.

And please laugh at yourself, rather than shame yourself if you do. We can only do better next time.

The Harm Caused When Our Actions Are Fueled by Negative Excitement

In Real's model of one-up/one-down and walled-off/boundaryless patterns, the "over-executive functionary" falls into the one-up, boundaryless category. When we find ourselves in this pattern, there is a part of us that believes we can do things better than those around us. That belief creates a form of negative excitement—another endorphin and oxytocin surge—that feels good in the moment.

When we act without being asked, however, we undermine the autonomy of others and harm both ourselves and those around us. In that moment, we are playing in the Human Grenade Playground.

Negative excitement can feel energizing, but it is not a healthy or sustainable pattern.

As we respond to one another's wounding patterns in this dance of life, I invite you to keep looking for the Win-Win Playground.

The Negative Effects of Denial

Denial is another common doorway into this playground.

When reality feels too threatening to face, the nervous system attempts to preserve safety by rejecting information, minimizing harm, or clinging to a simplified narrative. While denial offers temporary relief, it requires enormous internal energy to sustain. Over time, this drains vitality, erodes trust, and limits creativity. This is especially true when there is no accompanying practice of self-reflection, forgiveness, or love.

Denial narrows the field of possibility.

Awareness expands it.

When you find yourself seeing only one possibility moving forward, you have likely moved into the Human Grenade Playground. Know that this separation from reality has probably served you well in the past to protect you. Honor your survival patterns; they kept you alive and got you to where you are today. Remind yourself that here, now, as you are reading this book, you are safe. Spend some time opening to the bigger picture, realigning with love, and see what unfolds from a place of curiosity and wonder.

Asking your brain to step into curiosity and wonder, brings you out of stress and supports the right brain to come back online—showing you, once again, the bigger picture of your life. As you widen your lens to perceive what is possible, the creative choice that is just right for you has the opportunity to emerge into your awareness.

Hopelessness and the Human Grenade Playground

Hopelessness is an energetic pattern that emerges when we are one down and in deep disconnection from the energies of Love and Freedom. It is one of the most difficult human experiences there is.

In this state, we do not feel love in our lives, we do not feel like we have choice, and we often cannot see a way forward or out of the pattern. We may feel a deep sense of bitterness as we support those we love, engage in our work, and complete our daily tasks.

Take a moment here to tune into the places in your own life where you feel hopeless. Notice which maladaptive playground you become drawn to. It may be the Human Grenade Playground or one of the others. Take a deep breath and invite yourself into the possibility of loving connection.

We can connect to our self-love, the compassionate love of others, whether that is our pets, nature, or other humans, and we can connect to God's love, the love of the Angels and higher beings. In a hopeless state, we often have blocked our 2nd (self-love), 4th (compassionate love), and 6th (Divine love) chakras. Invite your chakras to open to the flow of love that surrounds us and that is within us. Open to receive Grace in your life. Grace is a gift that we can all access. We don't need to do anything but receive. Be compassionate with yourself, soften your armor, and know that this is a phase, and it too shall pass.

Dr. Upledger has stated, our trauma persists in isolation. Get some help, find friends or professionals to connect with. Open yourself up to receiving love and support both through tapping into your golden shadow qualities of beauty, agency, power and discernment. Eventually, compassionate love will emerge within your community for you. Open yourself to spaciousness and allow Plan B to emerge. Plan B will unfold in the right Divine time, in the right Divine way.

Make a single choice. Choose love. Let go of outcome. Step back into the Win-Win Playground.

Shame, Guilt, and Repair

Shame is another one of the densest energies we can hold when we move "one down" and walled off. It is attachment to the belief "I am bad." If we carry this belief and move into a boundaryless pattern, we harm ourselves and others: sometimes dramatically or sometimes quietly. The belief "I am bad" is held in our mental field, a yellow structural field of energy influenced by our thoughts.

Brené Brown has written extensively about the subtle and not-so-subtle ways shame shapes our lives. With humor and empathy, she offers a pathway back into the Win-Win Playground through humor, vulnerability and courage.

Guilt is different. Guilt says: I am acknowledging that did something (or didn't do something) that caused harm.

Guilt is a healthy response when we realize we have stepped out of alignment with the highest good of ourselves and others. It motivates us to do better with our next action moving forward.

Guilt can motivate repair. Jonathan Bessone, of Thriving Healers, states that healthy repair comes from the emotion "I am sad" rather than the belief "I am bad."

The next time you feel guilty, take a moment to check in. Is "I am sad" or "I am bad" a stronger message? **Shift from "Bad" to "Sad"** if necessary, before making repairs.

Terry Real, in his book *The New Rules of Marriage*, states that a healthy repair contains four elements, two external, and two internal. Outwardly, you name your behavior and acknowledge the impact. Inwardly, you limit any attempts to justify the behavior, and you wait to repair until you are out of defense and able to speak from your wise adult self.

From an energetic perspective, we do this by allowing love to flow from the heart chakra down into the solar plexus chakra. This love provides a container for the structural form of your solar plexus chakra to soften the rigidity created by the field of judgement and shift towards being a more flexible source of connection to your personal power. Then you can drop your awareness to your second chakra and let the sadness flow.

Our mind sees actions and creates stories about these actions in others. We have an emotional response to the stories we create. Likewise others are constantly creating stories about our actions and motivations and having an emotional response to the story they are creating. When those we love perceive harm, it is appropriate and relational to feel sad about the exchange. Our sadness and grief is a wonderful and healthy motivator for us to do better. When we are in healthy relationship with our sadness and feel the emergence and flow in our system, we start to gently use our sadness to form repair from a place of equality.

We can say: "I am sorry, I reacted that way. It was not my intention to harm you, and I hear that it did. Again I am sorry and I love you."

When this communication comes from the second chakra, it is felt as real. You are repairing while staying emotionally connected to yourself and others. When you say the same words while focusing on your third chakra, the sensation of the language feels manipulative and there is danger of the judgement of "I am bad" or "you are bad" to non-consciously taint the conversation. Getting stuck in the mental field of the 3rd chakra can lead to over functioning for others (one-up and boundaryless), chronic blame (one-up and boundaryless), or emotional cutoff creating false peace (one-up and walled off); all of which can limit healthy repair.

When you notice yourself in Human Grenade dynamics—whether "one-up" or "one-down"—the invitation is the same:

Breathe yourself back into heart centered connection. Soften your armor. Allow grace and your inspiration to reveal the next right step.

The opposite of Victim is Creator.

Remembering Our Shared Humanity

The Human Grenade Playground thrives on dehumanization—on forgetting that every person is navigating their own fears, wounds, and longing for safety and belonging.

When we widen our awareness, we begin to see how quickly the victim–persecutor–rescuer triangle can activate within us. Not as a moral failure, but as a nervous-system response.

Gently notice:

- Whether your breath has shortened

- Where lack of safety is presenting as tension in your body

- How quickly certainty and blame arises

Soften your gaze.

Return to the heart.

Reconnect with the larger field of love that holds us all.

Allow love to flow into the energy of forgiveness. Be with the creativity that the flow of forgiveness creates in your energetic field. Allow yourself to be grateful for the positive changes in your life. Your external world will shift and relate to you in a different way as your internal shift

As we become aware of our patterns—and through awareness gain greater access to choice—we must catch ourselves when we step into maladaptive playgrounds and return to the Win-Win.

For me, I tend to move first into the Masochist Playground, driven by over-giving fed by a sense of not being enough if I am not doing enough. Three weeks after surgery, I was making plans to fly to Florida to volunteer at a multi-hands CranioSacral Therapy program—until my nurse told me, solidly, "No," and explained that I was still at risk for blood clots if I flew too soon.

When my actions are fueled by false archetypal images of teacher, hero, super-mom, super-wife, I can pop into the Competitive Playground. When that pattern escalates into over-planning for others—followed by resentment for doing things no one asked me to do—I can get a little hysterical in my resentment, and I find myself squarely in the Human Grenade Playground.

I do my Ho'oponopono prayer (introduced in Habit #3) and re-align to the Win-Win Playground. Over time, realigning becomes easier. We habituate to the nourishing, expansive, creative energies of the Win-Win Playground, and we can play there for longer and longer periods. It takes bigger and bigger life events to move us back into one of the maladaptive playgrounds.

Returning to the Win-Win Playground is not just about our words and our sense of self in relation to others and the whole, it is about the actions that emerge out of our new internal landscape and how the external world changes in response. As we begin to see the world differently, from the lens of deeper love for ourselves and the whole, we respond differently in our interactions with others, and their response has the opportunity to change as well. We embody positive change and the world reacts.

The Gifts Hidden in the Human Grenade Pattern

The Human Grenade Playground is the most destabilizing of the four playgrounds. It is where fear mixes with love. Where urgency overrides discernment. Where boundarylessness replaces containment.

And yet—even here—there are gifts.

The Human Grenade pattern often arises in people who care deeply.

The energy behind it is not apathy.

It is intensity.

It is protectiveness.

It is a fierce desire for safety, justice, or belonging.

At its core, the Human Grenade pattern carries raw life force.

When fear floods the system and we lose containment, that life force explodes outward; words become weapons, certainty becomes righteousness, emotion becomes combustible.

But underneath the explosion is sensitivity.

Underneath the rage is heartbreak.

Underneath the urgency is longing.

The gift inside the Human Grenade Playground is passion unfiltered.

It is the part of us that refuses to be numb.

The part that cannot tolerate injustice.

The part that feels deeply—sometimes too deeply—for the body to hold without skill.

This energy, when integrated, becomes moral courage.

It becomes advocacy rooted in love rather than shame.

It becomes the ability to name harm without dehumanizing those who cause it.

It becomes the power to say:

"This matters. And we can address it without destroying one another."

Many social movements begin with Human Grenade energy. The problem is not the fire. The problem is the lack of containment.

Fire warms.

Fire cooks.

Fire purifies.

Uncontained fire destroys.

The same is true of our nervous systems.

When fear and anger move through a regulated body, they become clarity and boundary.

When they move through a dysregulated body, they become explosion.

The gift of the Human Grenade Playground is access to intensity.

The work is learning to hold that intensity inside a heart that remains open.

When we learn to stay present with our own activation — breathing, softening, grounding — we discover that we do not need to discharge our pain outward to feel relief.

We can metabolize it, and when we metabolize it, something extraordinary happens: intensity becomes presence.

Conviction becomes compassion.

Power becomes service.

The same life force that once scattered others can become the energy that gathers people toward healing.

This is not suppression.

This is transformation.

The Human Grenade energy is not wrong. It is simply uncontained love mixed with fear.

When fear is held in grace, what remains is fierce love.

And fierce love, anchored in humility, is one of the most powerful forces on the planet.

Tuning In (Not Out) to Return to the Win-Win Playground of Love and Equality

When I am contemplating a major decision, I state it clearly—as a statement, not a question—and feel into my body wisdom:

This is for my highest good and the highest good of the whole.

If my body responds with openness and ease to both parts of that statement, I say "yes" and trust that both internal and external resources are there to support me. If I feel contraction through increased tension or heaviness in my body—I pause and say "no", knowing that proceeding would likely take me into one of the maladaptive playgrounds.

I tune into this statement somatically because I have practiced for decades in listening to my body's wisdom. You may feel your response differently, through sensation, emotion, or a quiet sense of knowing. You might feel increased heart coherence, or access a clear inner intuition. You might hear the answer, sense joy, or touch the field of divine knowing that becomes available when you are deeply connected to God's love that holds us all.

There is no right way. What matters is that you learn to listen. As you practice, try finding two ways of listening that work for you, so you can build confidence in your own guidance as you get confirming responses from two senses. Keep Tuning In. Your Inner Wisdom will lead you towards wellness and into exploring higher frequency playgrounds in the right way and at the right timing for you. The goal is not to avoid the Human Grenade Playground, because in times of stress we all drop into it, the goal is to develop ease of vertical movement, so that when your defense patterns do become boundaryless, you can return to center and move back up to a higher frequency playground with ease.

Healthy Habit #3
Be The Light

When we are aligned, and vibrating at a cellular level, with the frequencies of love, honor, sadness, forgiveness and gratitude, we become positive change makers in the world simply through our state of being.

When we move out of this alignment, into judgement, fear, or shame, for example, our nervous system responds by becoming activated. This activation is the cue for us to make a change. Rather than allowing our activation to pull us into the Victim, Persecutor, Rescuer triangle; our tools of loving awareness, breath, and intention allow us to stay in heart coherence. For many years, I have worked with another tool: which is a variation of the Hawaiian Ho'oponopono practice. I repeat to myself:

I love me. I honor what is within. I am sorry. I forgive myself. I am grateful for the lesson.

The traditional Ho'oponopono prayer was introduced to me about fifteen years ago as a tool for working with some anger I was carrying at the time. This may sound strange to you, but as I tuned in somatically, what emerged was anger toward the medical staff present during my own birth. The story I had created around this is that the doctors induced my mother's labor process too soon resulting in my premature birth. In that moment, I believed I was supposed to send the prayer outward—and my entrenched inner Victim was not willing to extend forgiveness to my perceived persecutors. I was playing in the Human Grenade Playground.

A few years later, I heard the story of a Hawaiian psychiatrist who would sit in his office and read through the charts of his patients. As he read, he noticed his body's responses to the stories in front of him. He practiced Ho'oponopono by stating "I love you, I am sorry, forgive me, thank you." to clear the restriction patterns arising in his own tissues. The patients, receiving an energetic model of coherence and wellness, began to shift and heal—and many did.

What changed everything for me was realizing that the practice begins within.

Now, when something makes me uncomfortable—or someone in my vicinity is agitated—I notice my response to that agitation and I practice my version of Ho'oponopono prayer:

I love me.

I envision myself surrounded by a circle of my love and Divine love, coming together at the heart and coherently working together in my field.

I honor what is within.

I feel the physical, emotional, and mental discomfort emerging in my body wisdom. I accept it and invite it to become bigger and more present in my awareness.

I honor any guilt I am holding—and I feel into my sadness for what I may have done or not done that contributed to the situation—and say:

I am sorry.

I acknowledge the patterns I have been carrying, likely for some time. As the stuck energy begins to release and my field returns to flow, I say:

I forgive me.

I feel the softening of tissues and the opening of breath that follows as I tune into the healing energy of forgiveness.

I finish with:

I am grateful for the lesson.

I allow gratitude to amplify and integrate the change.

This practice clears internal restriction patterns and restores flow. And when we shift our internal field, the external world responds.

When I work on my own reaction to another's struggling, the change in my personal energy field and tissues, supports the change in their fields. I have witnessed agitation soften, fear dissolve, and healing unfold—not through force, but through presence.

Show up in love. Let go of outcome. Be the light.

This practice begins within us. Nothing needs to be sent outward for it to work.

So far, the path of becoming a positive change maker has invited three essential shifts.

First, we show up in love, soften our gaze and open to the Plan B that God holds for us—often far beyond what we can currently imagine. Second, we align our intentions with the Win-Win Playground, choosing actions that nourish both ourselves and the whole equally. Third, when discomfort arises in our tissues, emotions, or thoughts, we turn inward with kindness and practice:

I love me. I honor what is within. I am sorry. I forgive me. I am grateful for the lesson.

As love, honor, sadness, forgiveness, and gratitude begin to flow more freely, something important happens: space opens within us. And it is in this spaciousness that creativity naturally emerges—not as something we have to force or strive for, but as a living expression of alignment. With greater access to creativity, we begin to co-create in new ways, and the world around us starts to shift in response.

When inner space opens, creativity often follows—without effort.

This brings us to the next essential habit.

Healthy Habit #4
Make Time for Creativity

Creativity is not optional—it is how we co-create reality with God.

If you find yourself thinking:

"I am not creative."

Pause, and take a moment to notice how that thought is creating a tension pattern within you.

Place a hand on your heart, take a breath and allow love and honor to emerge.

Release it with *I love me. I honor what is within, I am sorry, I forgive me, I am grateful for the lesson.*

Creativity is a natural expression of life force. I often perceive it as golden bubbles rising from the core essence of my clients into the personal energy field. Creativity is the new way that emerges when we are deeply connected both to our core essence and to the spaciousness and softness in our energy fields that allows change to be integrated.

Creativity here is not performance.

It's permission.

Our personal process work is creative work. As we deepen our connection with the different levels of self—the Inner Physician supporting physical health, Inner Wisdom supporting emotional and mental health, and the Higher-Self supporting spiritual health—something essential unfolds. Our soul's involution (the inner drive to create from alignment) begins to mingle with our soul's evolution (God's grace feeding change from the field of oneness as we open to receive). As this integration occurs, our sense of what is possible—for ourselves and our communities—expands. We feel energized to take action as the change we wish to see in ourselves and in the world.

During my training at the Barbara Brennan School of Healing, students were required to engage in an annual creative project. One year, as part of my personal process work, I asked myself: *Was there anything I loved to do as a child that was dampened by my life experiences?*

The answer came immediately: singing.

I then asked a second question: *How might engaging in this creative project make my life and the lives of those around me even more wonderful?* I realized I wanted my Win-Win Playground to include greater access to wonder and a lived experience of miracles.

That same year, I felt drawn to explore how we manifest through the spoken word. Following curiosity is itself a creative act. I listened and re-listened to The Game of Life and How to Play It, by Florence Scovel Shinn, and began paying close attention to the language I used—both aloud and internally.

The energetic impact of our thoughts and our spoken words is the same within the personal energy field. This is why it matters to be conscious and loving with language. When you notice yourself slipping into old patterns of fear, shame, or judgment-laden language, gently return to the Win-Win Playground.

Notice how your body responds to the words you use. When contraction arises, use your Ho'oponopono practice to restore healthy flow. Language is not just communication—it is vibration.

Anyone who has attended church understands how the vibrational impact of words is magnified through singing, especially in community. Take time to sing. Give yourself the gift of engaging in whatever creative expression brings you bliss. Follow your curiosity. Follow your wonder.

Singing, art, movement, writing—these are not indulgences. They are acts of alignment. When we make time for connected creativity, we attune to Grace. Bliss ripples outward, and the world responds.

Here is the song I created that year to support my attunement to living in the matrix of wonder and miracles. It is a song-circle format—one person sings each stanza, and the group sings it back together:

I have a wonderful life.

And I live in a wonderful way.

I provide wonderful service.

And I receive more wonders each day.

We live in a wonderful community.

And we live in a wonderful way.

We play in wonderful service.

And we grow in love each day.

I have a wonderful work.

And I work in a wonderful way.

I provide wonderful service.

And I receive wonderful pay. [1]

We live on a wonderful planet.

And we live in a wonderful way.

We share in wonderful service.

And we receive love each day.

I have a wonderful life.

And I live in a wonderful way.

I receive wonderful service.

And I attune to grace each day.

Creativity is action through embodied alignment. It is not what we produce, or the mastery of our performance, that matters most. What matters is our connection to love, wonder, and the desire for change. As creativity opens us to new possibilities, it naturally invites curiosity. When we loosen fixation and allow wonder back into our lives, we begin asking deeper questions—not from fear, but from openness. Creativity does not simplify the human experience; it makes us more available to its complexity.

This brings us to the next essential habit: staying curious about why life unfolds as it does—especially in the realms of health, suffering, resilience, and meaning.

1

---

1. [1] This stanza comes from The Game of Life and How to Play It by Florence Scovel Shinn.

Healthy Habit #5
Stay Curious

Stay Curious About the Complexities of the Human Experience

Why do some people get sick while others seem to move through life without massive disruption? And why do some souls come into bodies riddled with pain from the start?

These are questions I have wrestled with—alongside the families I have served—for over thirty years. As a Pediatric Craniosacral and Occupational Therapist I have had the opportunity to witness a wide range of experiences and I have come to the conclusion: the answers are complicated, and rarely reducible to a single cause.

What I have witnessed, again and again, as a facilitator of healing is this: when it is the soul's desire to shift a pattern of dis-ease into a pattern of ease, the way forward often begins by going toward the source(s) of the dis-ease—with curiosity, not blame.

I had the privilege of serving as a teacher's assistant to Tad Wan-Veer, who created the Glial curriculum for the Upledger Institute. Tad WanVeer is a visual artist and one of the most beautiful models of humility-in-action I have ever met. He developed a system of images that helps the body wisdom of our clients communicate through right-brain image consciousness—so the tissues can project information directly to the therapist's image brain centers to support the therapist's role in facilitating healing.

WanVeer once shared a story of a young girl who was developing typically and then, suddenly over the course of one day and for unknown reasons, lost her ability to control her bodily movements except for her head, right arm, and hand. In addition, she lost her ability to speak, lost eye control, and developed epilepsy. Despite the severity of these challenges and after years of receiving various therapies, her family discovered that she was able to communicate through augmentative methods, allowing her to express her thoughts and feelings.

The girl's mother recounted to Tad that a friend of the family asked the little girl if she understood why these events had happened. In response, the girl shared a profound perspective:

"This sort of thing happens to me and other children to remind people that the world is made of love."

She did not become classically abled in the way the medical model might measure. She did become a brighter, clearer beacon of love—within herself and within her family. That story has stayed with me for years.

Getting Curious After the Surgery

On Christmas Eve 2025, I woke with burning pain in my gut. My husband brought me to the emergency room at six a.m. I was in surgery by one p.m. for a rupture of my sigmoid colon with an abscess, and in recovery by four that afternoon.

I spent the next thirteen days in the hospital on IV antibiotics, working to get my white blood cell count under control, and dealing first with a PV drain and then an IR drain to release persistent fluid buildup between my intestines.

That was a massive shift in my health. And within days, I found myself asking: "What were the sources of this event?"

Of course, our health is influenced by many factors: genetic predispositions, lifestyle choices, what we do and don't do, what we think and don't think (including the ways we limit our sense of what's possible), how we metabolize emotions, and external conditions such as family dynamics and environmental or chemical exposures.

On top of these are collective matrix stresses: such as the social trauma of middle-school bullying, oppression toward immigrants, people of color, and people with disabilities, and the countless ways society shapes the nervous system.

The list of factors that affect our health can seem endless, and science is now showing us even more layers. Epigenetics matters.

The egg that becomes you is formed while your mother is still in your grandmother's womb. So, what was happening in your grandmother's environment when she became pregnant with your mother impacts you. If your egg formed during famine, you may carry extra weight. If it formed during war, you may struggle with sleep. The factors are many, and they interact.

This is part of why curiosity is so essential. When we get fixated on only one pathway toward health, we get stuck.

Curiosity widens the field. Blame narrows it.

Sometimes we try to analyze our way out of a problem by trying to fix what is perceived as wrong when what our system would most benefit from is feeding into the energies of what is right. For example, we may become focused on a nutritional depletion and choose to add supplements. However, if we broaden our perspective on health, what our tissues might really want and what may bring our ability to absorb nutrients into a healthier range, is to access our internal sense of joy while moving creatively. (Please note, this is an example, not medical advice).

Sometimes the healing action is internal. Shifting perspective to notice and be with the felt sensations, emotions or images that come from the tissues. When we allow ourselves to become the images that our tissues are presenting within the container of love and connection, positive change occurs.

Sometimes the change needed is external—we may need to change something we are doing or not doing that is impacting our health. Or we may need to change our environment itself so that we have greater access to our core essence and internal sense of happiness that occurs with deep connection to self.

Happiness, in my experience, comes from a clear connection to core essence. It is not achieved through material gain, financial status, or even a romantic partner. Those things may come more easily once we are living more regularly in the Win-Win Playground and following our bliss—but they are not the source of our happiness. Our happiness and our joy are our natural states when we are aligned and connected to self as an equal member of the whole.

From Labeling to Listening

We label ourselves in countless ways: through job titles, diagnoses, personality frameworks, archetypes, and spiritual language. We also can label our experiences through repetitive stories about who we have been, what we have done, and what has been done to us.

Some labels are useful. They help us orient. They give language to experience. They create a shared understanding.

The problem is not labeling.

The problem is fixation.

There is a difference between playfully wearing a label and becoming fused with it.

When we play with identity, it is fluid. It expands and contracts. We can put on a persona and take it off when we are done with it. There is room for creativity in how we engage with the different aspects of ourselves.

When we fixate, the label hardens. It becomes an image we must live up to. And when we fall short of that image, shame can arise.

Curiosity keeps identity flexible.

Fixation turns identity into a cage.

Another kind of fixation I often see is when someone becomes attached to an external diagnosis or label and begins valuing outside guidance over inner guidance.

To restore inner access, soften your gaze, drop into body wisdom, and feel into what does not feel aligned in your environment.

When you are having a medical crisis, you want medical help. Diagnoses are extremely valuable. They give you information so your inner physician—the higher-self aspect of you in charge of your physical body—can make educated decisions alongside your medical team.

In the Win-Win playground, you are an equal member of your care team. Your Inner Physician is fully resourced. It knows what is best for you. Tune into that voice and let it speak as you negotiate what feels right for you.

My Mother's Story

My mother showed me a beautiful example of this.

At age seventy-two, she was diagnosed with breast cancer. Her biopsy revealed two types of cancer: the typical slow growing breast cancer found in older adults, and a more aggressive, fast growing breast cancer that startled the medical team.

It turns out that she, and I, carry a "BRCA Abnormal" gene. What is that? You might ask. It is so rare, that many physicians are unfamiliar with it. It includes a missing portion of the gene sequence that typically slows cancer growth.

When you receive news like that—a genetic abnormality, a heightened risk—it can be very easy to fixate on the diagnosis as destiny.

But genetics are not fate.

Gene expression is influenced by internal environment—stress and calm, nourishment and depletion—as well as external environment: food, air, water, relationships. Even the stress and resilience patterns of our ancestors and descendants influence expression.

The medical team recommended surgery, radiation and chemotherapy. My mother said *yes* to surgery and radiation and *no* to chemo. They also recommended a medication with significant side effects to be taken for the next ten years to reduce recurrence risk. She tuned inward and said, *"No thank you, I will take my chances."*

My mother turned ninety this spring.

This is not a story about rejecting medicine.

This is a story about listening inward rather than excepting generic external algorithms of care. Especially when we receive a frightening diagnosis, we need to stay in curiosity — balancing medical guidance with inner knowing.

State your needs.

Open yourself to receive support.

Explore what is emerging for healing.

Keep returning to love for yourself.

I truly believe that many of life's thresholds are invitations from our higher self—opportunities to deepen our capacity to love.

When you find yourself in a stressful situation, whether it is related to your health, money or relationships, avoid patterns of blame. Instead focus on staying curious. You can say *This is for me. What is here for me to learn?*

This statement is an incredibly powerful response to someone objectifying you. If you can detach from their objectifying statement or action, you regain your agency as the subject of your life.

Self-Labeling

Another way we get stuck is through labeling ourselves.

I was recently in Canada, precepting an advanced CranioSacral Therapy class in Niagara Falls, Ontario, when one student blurted out:

"I am a matrix issue!"

In that moment, I could feel the fixation form in her personal energy field.

She was thankfully able to work through it during her five days of personal process work.

When we say something as truth—"I am this"—we solidify a pattern. We reduce a multidimensional being into a single story.

When in the role of preceptor during advanced CranialSacral Therapy classes, I enjoy watching for group patterns that come into conscious awareness. That week, I noticed a habit forming: students offering each other comments as they got off the table such as "good job" or "that was beautiful." I could also feel how even positive judgment can pull someone away from core self and toward external referencing for gratification.

Eckhart Tolle has said that labels separate us from presence and reduce people to mental concepts. The moment we fix someone with a label, even a positive one—we stop meeting them where they are. I have noticed that labeling—even positively—can create subtle restrictions in the energy field of the client and pulls them out of the full internal experience of their process.

When working in teams, feedback is valuable. Just remember to name it as perspective rather than truth.

Instead of: "That was beautiful."

Try: "I experienced so much beauty in that process."

The difference is subtle—but powerful.

Chas Perry, PhD, Dean of the Advanced Curriculum for the Upledger Institute, often responds to deep process work with a simple:

"Wow."

I love that.

It honors wonder without imposing valuation. It allows the student or client to stay internally engaged as they integrate involution—the creative change emerging from core essence—with evolution—the creative change that is unfolding in response to the external/environmental pressures of God's love and grace in the biogenesis of body-mind.

Returning to Internal Referencing

Labels do serve a purpose. Diagnoses can be accurate. Roles can be useful.

It is attachment that restricts the field. When we cling to labels others give us, or to labels we give ourselves, we shift from internal referencing to external referencing.

We begin asking: "How am I doing? Am I measuring up? Do I fit the ideal image?"

Curiosity invites a different inquiry: "What feels true right now? What is my body telling me? What is emerging?"

Use labels lightly. Listen deeply.

Move beyond the label and find the path to wellness—whatever that means to you.

Seeking Support Without Seeking a Rescuer

As CranioSacral Therapists, we facilitate our clients process to open perspective and tune into their deep core self for the way forward. Through this process of widening and centering, they learn to bring non-conscious patterns into conscious awareness.

Dr. John E. Upledger called the part of us that is whole, healthy, and knows the way forward "the Inner Physician," and he wrote an excellent, easy-to-read book called *The Inner Physician and You* that I recommend wholeheartedly.

When we are working with spirituality, we might call that whole, knowing part the higher self, Holy Spirit, or inner God/Goddess-self. When we are working with body wisdom navigating the playgrounds, we might say Inner Wisdom or Deep Knowing Self. Again—stay flexible with labels.

Kat Placencio, who directed the Upledger Institute Clinic for many years and now runs dolphin-associated therapy programs through Integrative Intentions, likes to say:

"CranioSacral Therapists don't give advice."

There are now over 200,000 CranioSacral Therapists worldwide, and their ability to hold loving neutrality varies as widely as the human experience. In general, the more personal process work a therapist does, the greater their capacity to let go of outcome and hold presence while you engage your own process.

I have met brand-new therapists with one class under their belt who truly get it. I have also met therapists who completed advanced curriculum yet remain unaware of judgment patterns—or who hold a hidden agenda to "fix" others.

Persevere With Curiosity: Go Toward the Source

I invite you to reflect on the belief that it is someone else's job to fix you. Looking for a rescuer can easily place you into one of the maladaptive playgrounds. Realign by breathing yourself back into equal footing with others and the divine matrix. It is wonderful and often necessary to have a healing team as we age. I encourage you to look for professionals who understand that it is through tuning into your inner physician, that the right way forward will emerge. You are co-creating your wellness experience with the part of you that is already whole, healthy and knows the right way forward. Stay curious. Stay open to what wants to emerge from your core essence. Keep searching until you find the support that is right for you.

And remember: it doesn't have to be a CranioSacral Therapist. Dr. Upledger also said, "Illness persists in isolation," and "If we could do this by ourselves, we would have our own planet." Seek the help you need so you can stay in the Win-Win Playground of life.

Curiosity is how we stop collapsing into blame, fixation, and false certainty. It widens the lens. It returns us to listening—listening to body, to image, to spirit, and to the many layers that shape a life.

There comes a moment when curiosity naturally asks for its next step, not more analysis, not more story loops, not more theories. Contact is required—a willingness to go closer to what is true, to what is held in the tissues, to what is carried in the lineage, and to what is waiting beneath the surface of a symptom. Curiosity brings us to the new way that is waiting to emerge in our lives at the timing that is right for us.

This is where the next habit begins: Go to the Source.

Healthy Habit #6
Go to the Source

One thing about being in the hospital on IV antibiotics for thirteen days is that you have a lot of time to contemplate life. As I tuned into my body and grew curious about the source of my colon rupture, I felt that the genetic component was the primary source of this event. My mother had undergone the same surgery at around the same age and recovered fully.

As a young adult, I created a story about my mother: that her angelic presence—I don't have a single memory of my mom expressing a negative thought about someone—had disconnected her from truly listening to her body, and that this pattern contributed to her colon rupture and later the removal of her gallbladder.

I see now that this story stemmed from a belief I no longer hold: the belief that if something "bad" happens, someone must be to blame or deficient in some way. That was not my body's truth. It was a lens of perception I carried at the time.

Touching the Somatic Source

When my colleague DeAnna Castleberry, CST-T, visited me in the hospital, we tuned in together to the somatic expression of the source of the rupture in my sigmoid colon. DeAnna offered feedback that there was a lot of frenetic energy in my prefrontal cortex. As I dropped down into my body, we both noticed the effort it took for me to truly be there.

We explored that pattern of effort, and what emerged was an image of vast emptiness in the lower left side of my pelvis. This is where the rupture had occurred. I identified it as ancestral, and DeAnna asked, How many generations back does it go?

I kept counting until I landed at 346 generations. When I moved to 347, the image and sensation left my body. Returning to generation 346, I explored what was there.

This was not about answers. It was about contact.

A sense of frustration arose—something like an ancient agreement within human consciousness: that as a species we would learn through Love and Freedom on this planet. As I tuned deeper, I felt discontent about the amount of suffering that would result from that choice.

I did my Ho'oponopono prayer:

I love me. I honor what is within. I am sorry. I forgive myself. I am grateful for the lesson.

And a pattern cleared.

DeAnna asked if there was something deeper. As I tuned in again, I felt rage. The rage had been pushed into the left side—into the area where my bowel had ruptured.

When our tissues present an image, one healing strategy is to become the image: to drop in somatically and notice, with curiosity, what a circle of love, and the intention to align with the highest good, does with what is present.

As I became the rage without judgement, it shifted toward my center and mixed with the golden light of my core essence, feeding my lower Tan Tien. (The lower Tan Tien is the energy center that is considered the source of life force and vitality in Chinese medicine.)

What I experienced was profound and difficult to put into words. My sense of self changed for the better.

A limiting belief shifted: from *rage is bad* to *rage and outrage can fuel positive change when held in the container of love.* Rage can be strong fuel for good when it is held within the Win-Win matrix.

Rage as Fuel, Not Fire

Anger, rage, charge and activation, when flowing, are signals from the nervous system that change is needed. Passion for change is powerful. This passion arises when we begin to notice what is out of alignment with our highest good and the highest good of all.

In the Win-Win Playground, rage fuels action as positive change makers. In the other quadrants, rage can scorch us—and those around us.

My mother-in-law carries a strong charge around budget cuts to universities and the National Science Foundation, and she is part of a political group working to respond. She spends ten hours a week cold calling citizens to support getting out the vote in swing states. Her outrage fuels her action for positive change.

For me, the reality that children are born into bodies of pain and struggle enrages me—and I do something about it. I have dedicated my career to develop the tools to support newborns to start their journey as regulated and healthy as possible. The rage motivates me to keep learning more.

Rage can fuel us. When we combine rage with love, we are energized to be positive change makers. Rage in the Masochist, Competitive, or Human Grenade playgrounds has enormous destructive potential. Be aware. Stay in the Win-Win Playground. Use your rage for good.

Rage vs. Negative Excitement

Energetically, I want to differentiate rage from negative excitement.

Rage is grounded. It can feel like it rises from the core of the planet—like a bright red ball of light at the Earth's center. When our deeper self is coherently connected to the deeper self of the planet, this red light flows through the root chakra. In times of creative passion, we may even perceive a bright red glow around the auric field.

When we remain in maladaptive playgrounds for too long, the red glow becomes darker, stagnant and sticky.

When we are coherently connected to the planet and perceive something out of alignment with the highest good of all, the red light still flows—and it can be experienced as rage or anger. In coherence, it becomes fuel for action.

Negative excitement is different. It often emerges through complaining. It is frenetic, primarily in the mental field, and has a stuck quality. When you move into negative excitement, it can feel good—there can be an oxytocin "dump" in the brain that becomes addictive.

When negative excitement becomes habitual, it can lead to analysis paralysis. We separate mind from the wholeness of body wisdom. We place the mind "one up" over the body, or the left brain "one up" over the right brain, and we miss the bigger picture. Over time, this pattern can contribute to health issues.

Other Lives Clearing and Working with Limiting Beliefs

During her second visit, DeAnna tuned into the possibility that the pattern held for 346 generations might also be connected to other lives. She asked me to tune into that.

My belief at that time was that the soul has multiple experiences across multiple lives (and possibly multiple dimensions). The soul exists outside of time and space, on the soul level, all these experiences are occurring together—perhaps hundreds of thousands of experiences happening at once. This is why I prefer the term *other lives* to *past lives*. The term, *other lives,* includes the multi-dimensional aspect of the soul's experience.

We can create a representational image to support us to work with the energies of our other lives. First, we ask the question: "Are there any other lives impacting this life?" Then we feel into our tissues for the response. If there is an increase in tension, your body is saying "yes." We then invite an image to emerge. The image that works for me, is the image of a menorah like candelabra, with candles extending in each direction to infinity. A lit candle means there is a connection between another life and my current process, and an unlit candle means that there is no connection. When the candelabra is facing up, I know that there are other lives that will benefit from the clearing and upgrading of energy in my current processing work. As I do my work, I invite these other lives to receive the positive change. When the candelabra is facing down, I go into receivership and receive the clearings that are going on in my other lives that are supporting me in this life. When I work with my clients, and they bring up other life work, I will often see this image as well.

During my session with DeAnna, I brought up the image of my candelabra that shows me the other lives in need of this healing and went into allow, clearing for all but two lives. Going into allow is the process of opening for energy and information to flow where it needs to flow for the highest good without being restricted by your mind maps—your need to understand the process.

As I explored one of the two remaining lives, I felt great pressure on my chest. Sometimes it's important to understand what a pressure is about. Sometimes a restriction can clear without detailed exploration through the Ho'oponopono practice.

With other lives, the core restriction is often a limiting belief brought into this life. A belief is different than a thought. A thought is held in your mental field, which is your yellow structural field monitored by your solar plexus chakra. Our thoughts and words affect our sense of agency and our intentional line of energy. A belief is more of a spiritual framework that effects the golden structural field monitored by your crown chakra. A limiting belief is any belief that is causing a restriction pattern in your field and is limiting your ability to be expansive. As I tuned in, the limiting belief revealed itself:

Love comes with sacrifice (loving you fully means depleting myself). I moved myself back into alignment with the Win-Win matrix and with my breath opened to the new way of being. As I felt my tissues and energy field shift, the new belief emerged: *My love nourishes myself and others fully and equally.*

The final life still feels "on hold." I still feel it in my left shoulder as I write this. I trust it will release at the right divine time. I remain curious. I remain patient. I hold compassion for myself.

Collective and Lived Experience

Collective One-Up Dynamics—Win at Any Cost in Politics

Over the last several years, I have witnessed both Democrats and Republicans in the United States make decisions from a "win at any cost" orientation. For example, when Democrats fund radical Republican candidates during primaries to improve their chances in the general election, they are playing in the Competitive Playground—harming the whole by limiting voters' access to centrist choices.

Republicans, in turn, have started openly admitting they are redistricting solely for the purpose of winning, with Democrats retaliating in kind. These are classic "tit-for-tat" Competitive Playground dynamics that erode trust and freedom and take away choice from American voters.

We can do better as a nation. What truly makes America great is not domination, but our commitment to love and freedom.

If you feel a charge rising, that makes sense. Take a slow inhale and let your exhale be slightly longer—we're not here to blame, we're here to see patterns clearly, so choice can return.

Let the breath widen your lens before we look at how "one-up" group dynamics can become contagious.

The Addictive Qualities of Collective Judgement

We take on the role of the one-up judger when we lose awareness of our shared humanity and the interconnectedness of our communities. When we inhabit this role, we often seek out others who share our values and reinforce our certainty.

We feed on the feel-good chemistry of negative excitement created through complaining and labeling. The brain releases oxytocin when we feel superior, and more oxytocin when we bond with like-minded people. Over time, this chemical loop can make one-up group identification feel regulating—and even addictive.

Before looking at how these dynamics operate at a national level, I want to name how easily "one-up" thinking becomes embedded within political parties. Members of both the Democratic and Republican parties engage in name-calling and broad negative labeling of the "other."

According to the Pew Research Center, majorities in both parties view members of the opposing party as more immoral, dishonest, and closed-minded than other Americans. Common Republican labels for Democrats include "corrupt," "unpatriotic," "radical," "lazy," and "out of control." Democrats often apply similar labels to Republicans, with "corrupt" and "extreme" among the most frequent, along with "unintelligent," "out of touch," and "hypocritical."

Positive labels used to describe one's own party function as a subtler form of separation. They create an oxytocin boost for those who strongly identify with the group, while implicitly suggesting that those outside the group possess the opposite qualities.

In the same 2022 Pew study, 67% of Republicans described themselves as "more hard-working" than other Americans—implicitly framing Democrats and non-voters as lazy. Meanwhile, 74% of Democrats described themselves as "more open-minded" than Republicans and non-voters, implying that those outside their group are closed-minded. Since 2016, the percentage of people in both parties who feel comfortable applying negative traits to members of the other party has risen sharply.

Let's bring this out of statistics and into lived experience—into something most of us recognize in our bodies.

We have all seen the "one-up" bully dynamic in school systems. Typically, a group of "cool kids" bands together and decides that an individual or group is so far down the social totem pole that they deserve cruelty. Often, those "cool kids" carry their own unhealed wounds. As a group, they find power through collective one-up identity. They create hierarchical "power-over" systems and take on the role of bully.

Unfortunately, this dynamic is now playing out with significant energy on a national scale.

A clear example is political messaging that depends on identifying an "other" to blame. Slogans that suggest someone has damaged our country require the creation of a group deemed "one down." The slogan Make America Great Again reinforces one-up thinking by implying that there are people actively destroying America.

Our current administration has labeled immigrants, the Queer community, people who are accused of "faking" disability, and the poor as one-down groups. This behavior is not new—it is simply louder and more emboldened in the current political climate.

Ava DuVernay's film, *Origin*, explores Isabel Wilkerson's work on how governments have historically used one-up systems to consolidate power and extract resources. From the caste system in India, to post-slavery dehumanization of Black Americans, to the targeting of Jews, Roma, artists, intellectuals, and the queer community in Nazi Germany, the pattern is consistent: when societies create "untouchable" groups, cruelty becomes easier to justify—and fear becomes easier to monetize.

This is a classic "power-over" strategy: taking more than one's share of resources from the whole.

The wealthiest Americans continue to get wealthier.

But at what cost?

Take one breath here. Let that question land without forcing an answer.

I invite you to contemplate with me a few of the bully tactics playing out in America today. What I describe—or what I choose not to include—may activate your nervous system. This list is not meant to be exhaustive. It is offered to support awareness of how conditional belonging harms individuals and communities.

As you read the sections that follow, use your tools of breath, present-time awareness, and the Ho'oponopono prayer to regulate activation and return to love. We will pause for nervous system check-ins and gentle resets after each Bully Tactic section.

The motivations behind policies that support these bully tactics—and the ways society absorbs and normalizes them—are complex. When policies arise from the Competitive Playground, resources are shifted—often financial resources—from the general population to a smaller, one-up group.

As long as this group remains in the Competitive Playground, resources are taken without regard for the impact on the "untouchable" groups that have been created. And when fear-based rhetoric is accepted at a societal level, harm scales—affecting not only disenfranchised communities, but all of us.

Societal Bully Tactic #1: Immigrants

The harm of being told you are no longer welcome

I am an immigrant. The current messaging of the Republican Party harms me.

When I hear Donald Trump say he wants the power to take away people's citizenship if they were not born in this country, my system drops into worry. My mind creates stories about a random administrator deciding that what I write here is "anti-American" and revokes my citizenship. I imagine my nearly three decades of service to this country will be ignored. When I go into deep patterns of worry, I lose sleep. So I do not harm myself too deeply, I do my Ho'oponopono prayer and return to love.

I am friendly with one of the political families in New Mexico. This young, loving couple—rather than simply celebrating that their child was old enough for daycare so they could return to work full-time—became so anxious in response to anti-immigrant rhetoric that they obtained a passport for their toddler son and placed a copy in his diaper bag.

Daycare providers remain among the lowest-paid workers in America, and many positions are filled by immigrants. With increased ICE raids, this family felt they needed an added layer of protection for their son because he is a person of color. Despite being U.S. citizens—and related to a Senator—they felt their child was at risk because he looks like he *could* come from an immigrant family.

Negative rhetoric harms us all: citizen or immigrant, white or brown, rich or poor.

I was born in Canada and moved to the U.S. legally when I was twenty-five. I am educated and white. I was not fleeing persecution. I did not have to leave my family because of lack of options. I was in the fortunate position of wanting an adventure—and being called to New Mexico. I was lucky enough to have a professional degree in a field where there was a shortage of staff so I qualified for a work visa. Within three weeks, I met the man who would become my husband. It was meant to be, we recently celebrated our 25th wedding anniversary.

During my recent hospital stay in Sacramento, it seemed to me that close to 80 percent of my direct care staff were immigrants. One woman who was born in South America measured my colostomy output and literally cleaned up my poop with a good attitude. She told me about her three sons—all first-generation Americans—one an engineer, one a Marine, and one a lawyer.

The attending surgical physician checking in on me was a Middle Eastern immigrant who trained in my hometown and gave me referrals to excellent surgeons back home for follow-up care. The interventional radiologist who came in on a Sunday to remove my drain—so I could finally be discharged—was also a Middle Eastern immigrant. He had earned a PhD in Electrical Engineering and worked at NASA before realizing he wanted to become a doctor. With his wife's support, he returned to school and followed his calling.

Making broad policy decisions that cut off immigrants—especially from universities and professional pathways—harms America.

A great America is an educated America.

We are fortunate when people like those above choose to build their lives here.

Before we move on, pause for one breath. Notice your jaw, your chest, your belly. Soften what you can—and come back to now. Let your heart stay online.

Societal Bully Tactic #2: The Queer Community

The harm of being told you are deviant for being different

Mental health struggles among youth in the non-cis community are occurring at an epidemic scale. When young people are told—explicitly or implicitly—that their identity is wrong, dangerous, or shameful, their nervous systems absorb that message deeply. This messaging is not new, but it is also not right. When administrations cater to the conservative Christian right for financial reasons, they are harming our society.

In response to the increasing negative rhetoric towards the queer community, older, wiser, and more resourced non-cis citizens are increasingly taking their intellectual property, their creativity, and their wealth and saying "no" to these bullying dynamics. Some are leaving the country altogether for places that welcome, nourish, and support them. The resulting Brain-Drain is hurting our society.

Both of these realities harm our country.

When we push people out—emotionally, socially, or geographically—we lose brilliance, innovation, and love. We fracture the field of connection that allows a society to thrive. A nation rooted in freedom cannot flourish while telling some of its citizens that they're very being is unacceptable.

Before we move on, pause for one breath. Notice your jaw, your chest, your belly. Soften what you can—and come back to now. Let your heart stay online.

Societal Bully Tactic #3: The Disabled

The harm of being told you are not enough

When I first moved to the United States, I was struck by the phrase "pull yourself up by your bootstraps." It is not a common phrase in Canada. Over time, I have reflected deeply on both its strengths and its limitations.

There is a positive message embedded in it: persevere, access grit, follow your dream. And there is also a subtle separation within it—a disconnection from interdependence—that places it squarely in Competitive Playground dynamics. It is commonly used to suggest that the best upward mobility is upward mobility that is created without outside help.

What if you were born without hands? What if you have a muscular disorder and do not have the strength? What if the movement is too painful? What if you lack the executive functioning to organize the steps of the task at hand?

The phrase can quietly communicate: you are a failure. You don't fit the ideal. You are not enough. There is deep irony in this statement. Historically when the phase was introduced into American culture, it was used to create an image of an impossible task. Our forefathers knew something that we obviously have forgotten—you can not succeed without help.

The belief—that independence is the highest value—harms the souls born into bodies that require interdependence in order to thrive.

My oldest child was born by C-section due to a footling breech position and has received physical therapy for most of their life. They walk with a cane and live with ADHD and autoimmune issues that create frequent strains in their joints. They graduated high school with eighteen college credits, earned a Presidential Scholarship to the University of New Mexico, and graduated on the Dean's List.

They do well walking two miles a day. At three miles, they require a recovery day. They work in a supportive environment and are saving for graduate school in Audiology so they can graduate debt-free.

Disability is complex.

There are many jobs my child cannot do. They may not be able to work full-time over the long arc of life, depending on how their autoimmune patterns evolve.

They are not "one down."

I, as a neurodivergent person who struggles with sensory processing and requires a high level of self-care, am not "one down." Nonverbal children on the autism spectrum are not "one down."

We are all God's children. Every soul, every core essence, is equally important in the Win-Win Playground.

Take a moment to pause for one breath. Notice your jaw, your chest, your belly. Soften what you can—and come back to now. Let your heart stay online.

Societal Bully Tactic #4: The Poor

The harm of believing poverty equals laziness and moral failure

There is strong negative rhetoric in our culture about the poor—framing them as "cheating the system," being lazy, or needing mandates to force engagement. Recent policies have been created that people must be in school, volunteering, or working a certain number of hours to retain benefits, or risk losing them.

Much of this rhetoric is rooted in a false belief: If you are poor, you must be lazy.

In America, there is a cultural anger toward the poor that I did not experience growing up in Canada. In some regions, people living in poverty are viewed as failing society—unwilling to "pull themselves up by their bootstraps."

For as long as I have lived in New Mexico, it has ranked as one of the highest States with respect to poverty. For twenty years, I worked in Early Intervention as an Occupational Therapist, with a birth to three years of age home-visiting program for families raising children with disabilities. I came to know many families living in poverty, and what became unmistakably clear is this:

Poverty is complicated:

- Some parents had learning differences and were doing their best.

- Many families were raising more than one child with a disability.

- Single parents often carried enormous caregiving loads with little support.

- Some parents were disabled.

- Some struggled with addiction or were dealing with the strain of multi-generational patterns of addiction within their extended family.

- And it was rare to encounter a family—whatever their circumstances—that did not love their children deeply and want the best for them.

Creating mandates that ignore the realities of caregiving, disability, trauma, and complex family systems does not fall into the Win-Win Playground.

Take a breath. The next section moves from analysis into lived experience. Let yourself listen with tenderness.

Norma's Story

While in the hospital, Norma (I have changed Norma's name for her privacy) and I shared a room as we healed from our individual ailments. She and I spent many hours talking, praying, and manifesting support together. She has given me permission to share her story.

Norma had her first sickle cell flare at age six and has lived with varying degrees of pain ever since. She works closely with her doctors, takes daily medication, attends church regularly, and volunteers at an animal shelter when her body allows.

She lives independently on disability payments. Those payments are not enough to purchase a car, so she relies on buses and family support to attend medical appointments, get her groceries and volunteer with the dogs at the local shelter. One of the most painful things she shared with me was the ongoing stress of societal judgment—of being both poor and disabled. Many people do not treat Norma well.

We must stop placing ourselves in a one-up position over people like Norma.

She is intelligent. She is capable. She is loving. She is poor.

These truths coexist.

Despite her limited income, Norma saved enough to fly to California to visit her brother and his family for the holidays. She bought her tickets far in advance to secure the best price. During her visit, she became ill and was admitted to the hospital with me as doctors worked to manage her sickle cell flare and pain.

She faced a painful reality: she was supposed to fly home, but her body was not yet well enough. She did not have the funds to easily change her ticket. I supported her in softening, reconnecting to God's love and grace, and opening to Plan B.

A friend reached out and showed her a car listed on Craigslist—well maintained, with new tires and a recent inspection. The owner was asking $5,000, and Norma negotiated the price down to $4,200.

My first reaction to the idea of her buying a car unseen was fear. What if she was being scammed? I paused, breathed, and checked in with higher guidance.

I made the statement: It is for Norma's highest good and the highest good of the whole for Norma to buy this car.

I received a clear yes for both.

We praised God for the Win-Win Playground manifesting in her life. This single decision would solve two problems at once: she would not need to spend her remaining funds on another plane ticket, and she would gain greater independence—reducing her reliance on others when pain or weather made the bus unrealistic.

Disability support systems are complex. Without going deep into policy or labels, what matters here is this: the structure can be punishing. It often makes saving nearly impossible. Resources are capped at levels that do not reflect modern reality. The current asset cap for a disabled person is $2000. If they save more than that, they risk losing their benefits. Despite inflation, this asset cap has not changed since 1989.

Norma saved carefully to visit her family, spent her savings on the trip, became ill, and found herself stranded.

On the day I was discharged, Norma asked her uncle—who is a minister at a megachurch in Memphis—for help purchasing the car. Like me, he may have felt fear about buying a vehicle unseen and did not immediately say yes. Norma sensed the flow around this opportunity and asked him to at least speak with the owner and get a feel of the vehicle for clarity. At the time, he did not step forward to act on her request.

Creating Space in Our Lives for God's Will

In the days after my discharge, I texted and tried to call Norma. She was constantly on my mind. Our shared hospital experience had bonded us in a way that felt sacred.

I received no response. I assumed her phone had died, that her uncle had come through, and that she was driving home.

On the seventh day, Norma finally reached out to me.

After I left the hospital, she had been alone. With no one in her extended family stepping forward, she used the last of her money to purchase a plane ticket home. While waiting for a taxi to the airport, she collapsed and was admitted to the ICU with pneumonia.

She spent five days in the ICU before being transferred to a rehabilitation hospital, where she regained access to her phone. During those five days, I was the only person who reached out to check on her.

Still, Norma—who is full of grace—continued singing her gospel music. She expressed gratitude that at least one person was holding her in love.

The original car had not yet been sold, so I created a GoFundMe account, seeded it with a $1,000 donation, and encouraged her to reach out to family and friends for support.

I truly believed this would become a healing moment—that her family and community would come together. Every $25 donation matters. Small acts, woven together, can create real support.

What happened next is painful to write.

When Norma reached out to her two sisters-in-law, both responded with some version of: "If you had given me more notice, I could have helped."

She then reached out to her church and spoke with the wife of the other Pastor—an elder in the congregation. The Pastor's wife told Norma the church has an emergency fund—but that it is reserved for people in greater need.

Norma replied, "I am stranded across the country with $77 to my name. How can anyone be in greater need than me right now?"

The woman laughed, told her to pray about it, and suggested she consider getting a job.

Norma responded without bitterness. She said, "I'm not even mad. But now I know—they are not my family. You are my family. You were the only one there for me in my time of need."

I told her I was willing to be angry on her behalf.

This anger fuels this book. This anger invites all of us to do better.

If you feel heat, sadness, or tightness as you read this, pause. Let your exhale lengthen. Let your heart hold the truth without collapsing into it.

With some distance, I can also see that this collective "no" became clarifying for Norma. It lifted a veil. Not because she deserved cruelty—but because the truth became undeniable: she could no longer pretend that she was being held in love by her current community.

And when we see clearly, we can choose differently.

This became an invitation for Norma to step into an upgraded self—one who chooses the Win-Win Playground, where she is not only guided in how to serve others, but also supported to receive God's grace and love equally and fully.

Because I do have strong family support, I became a temporary bridge for her—inviting her to play with me in a field where we are both nourished, and where everyone has exactly what they need.

There is a soft, luminous connection between us now. Although I acted as a bridge, we stand on equal ground. Our time together—and the way we supported one another—felt gently facilitated by something larger than either of us. It felt like we were being connected by Angels.

Let's take what we've just witnessed and look at the mechanism of change: how spaciousness invites Plan B.

Plan B and the Cellular Shift

Plan B often arrives when the vibration at the level of our cells shifts upward. This shift occurs when we invite spaciousness into our personal energy field. Spaciousness softens the fixations that keep us rigidly bound to old patterns and familiar outcomes.

For Norma, I believe this cellular and energetic shift occurred when she opened to the possibility of not returning to Memphis, but instead moving to Albuquerque.

For those familiar with Barbara Brennan's work, this spaciousness corresponds to the fifth level of the personal energy field, which is associated with the throat chakra. The fifth level is the field of Divine Will. (See Barbara Brennan's illustrations in *Hands of Light*, or available images online.) When we open to spaciousness at this level, we open to Divine Will working in our lives in mysterious and often transformative ways. From this place, everything can change.

Over the next few days, Norma and I remained in communication with the owner of the original car. He raised the price back to $4,200, declined to deliver the vehicle to the hospital, and repeatedly avoided providing the VIN so I could verify the car's history and arrange insurance.

Eventually, he told me the car had been sold to someone else.

At that point, I wondered whether there might be a Plan C. I began exploring the possibility of purchasing a train ticket for Norma to New Mexico and reassessing next steps, knowing that the train did not travel all the way to Tennessee.

If your system is tracking this like a stress story, pause for a breath. Stay with the arc: contraction often comes before a shift.

By this time, Norma was resonating solidly in the Win-Win Playground. She had made a clear decision: she was moving to the higher-frequency environment of New Mexico, and she was getting a car.

Within hours, she found a single-owner vehicle with a clean title and a VIN—for $2,500. The owner, Andy, was willing to deliver the car directly to the hospital. This amount closely matched what we had raised in the GoFundMe account I had created with the support of my family and friends.

I checked in with the statement: *It is for Norma's highest good and the highest good of the whole to buy this car.*

The answer was a clear yes.

By midafternoon, Norma had the keys, title, and bill of sale in her hands. The car was parked outside the hospital. I had arranged the insurance.

Now we needed to solve the final piece: food, gas, and lodging for the sixteen-hour drive from Sacramento to Albuquerque.

Norma had been lamenting that no one from her old community

had supported her. I gently invited her to stay present and look around for who was stepping up now.

She reached out to the nursing staff and asked for support—and for a Bible. She was given two $50 gas cards, the Bible, and informed that upon discharge they would send her with multiple packed lunches for the journey.

Looking for who is stepping up in the present moment, and meeting that support with gratitude, helps keep us aligned in the Win-Win Playground.

The decision to leave her old community was transformational for Norma. That environment had kept her in a tightly sealed box—no light coming in, no light going out. They could not see her as the beautiful, radiant child of God that she is.

The Divine works in mysterious ways. As Norma steps out of that box and allows her light to shine as an equal member of God's family, her choice will ripple outward and impact the people she leaves behind.

By saying "no" and leaving, she creates an energetic void in her former community. Whenever a void is created, there is an opportunity for God's love and grace to enter and bring change to the larger system.

Her choice becomes a model for transformation. This is made even more powerful by her willingness to walk away from the community that consistently devalued her.

Jesus said, "You will know them by their works." As you step into the Win-Win Playground, look for playmates who meet you in loving connection. Say no—and walk away—from those who remain habitually stuck in maladaptive playgrounds.

Let this land as an invitation, not a demand. Your timing matters.

For those who are on the edge of a playing field and who are showing some curiosity about healthier ways to live, we become a bridge to the Win-Win playground, not by giving unsolicited advice, but by modeling love in action in our own lives.

The Intuitive, Lee Harris, in his January 2026 Podcast with Pam Gregory suggests that on a planetary level, roughly 25–30% of us are now actively choosing love over fear. This means that more and more of us are being called to serve as bridges—not through effort or force, but through our state of being.

We are saying *no* to fear-based media. We are saying *no* to feeding relationships that restrict and deplete us.

In many dysfunctional systems, there is a tipping point—when one person's awareness shifts, the veil lifts, and they choose to walk away. They step into a higher-vibrational playground. They choose to love themselves as equal members of the whole.

And in doing so, they quietly change the world.

Integration and Practice

A Collective Invitation Back to the Win-Win

When fear-based rhetoric is used to create separation, it can pull us toward the Competitive and Human Grenade playgrounds. I want to be clear: this is not about political party-bashing. The reality of politics, in every country across the world, is that it is all too easy to slip into maladaptive playgrounds because of the win-lose nature of the political game.

I do believe, however, that some leaders consciously use one-up bullying dynamics because they understand the neuroscience of fear and motivation. Niccolo Machiavelli asked the question, "How does a leader maintain power in an imperfect world?" He supported the use of fear—without cruelty—to control a population and maintain power. He wrote during a time of civil unrest, assassinations, and widespread upheaval.

Across the globe, we as humans are collectively saying no to cruelty, both subtle and overt. Old regimes are toppling, and young people across the planet are demanding fairness. For those in positions of power, the deeper Win-Win question becomes: *How does a leader maintain integrity, effectiveness and human connection without abandoning love?*

Sustainable leadership requires the courage to move beyond domination and into relational integrity. Win-Win leadership is not the absence of boundaries, discernment, or strategic thinking. It is holding the intention of seeking the highest good of yourself and the whole as you discern the right action within an imperfect system. It is the refusal to abandon the humanity of yourself and others in pursuit of outcome. It is the willingness to hold a broader awareness: that with each decision, we are balancing our highest spiritual good, our highest physical good, the highest spiritual good of the whole, and the highest physical good of the whole in our intentional energetic body.

As leaders, we acknowledge, that often we are making *good enough* decisions. And when fear seeps in—as it frequently does, sometimes with disastrous consequences—our journey as spiritual beings includes increasing our capacity to bring our non-conscious fears into our conscious awareness and to forgive ourselves. We adjust our actions, and continue to expand the circle of love in our energetic fields.

By working with our somatic signals of dis-alignment, we deepen our trust in ourselves as equal members of the whole. As we strengthen our connection to the messages being communicated through the physical self, in my experience, we also deepen our trust in the evolutionary process of love flowing within the whole.

I invite anyone in positions of power—local, state, or national—to pause, breathe, and notice what is happening in your body as you make policy decisions.

If you feel constriction, use the Win-Win Ho'oponopono prayer:

I love me. I honor what is within. I am sorry. I forgive me. I am grateful for the lesson.

America does not need to be made great again. America is already great—especially when we remember the freedom our culture aspires to protect. More and more of us are beginning to look inward instead of outward as we make authentic choices that are right for us within the framework of kindness. We are stepping away from decision-making fueled by fear, and returning to choices grounded in authentic connection and love. We are letting creativity flow in the playground of individuated equality, which mirrors the equality of the whole.

Anyone can choose to step out of the one-up playground and into the Win-Win field. I invite that choice. I see the core essence in each of you. It is strong, beautiful, and bright.

When you notice yourself moving "one up," pause. Feel your heart. Reconnect with the abundant field of love that holds us all, and breathe yourself back down to equality.

When you notice yourself moving "one down" pause. Feel your

heart and breathe yourself back up to equality.

A simple affirmation can help:

The love in you is as important as the love in me.

We are all God's children.

We all deserve to play in the Win-Win Playground.

When we are stressed, those of us with one-up tendencies tend to move into one of two states: one up and walled off (the Competitive/Judgmental Playground) or one up and boundaryless (the Human Grenade Playground). Both arise from disconnection from a heart-centered relationship with God's love and grace—in ourselves and in the whole.

As we become aware of these patterns in our lives, we breath ourselves back to equality and connection by focusing on our hearts.

A Meditation to Support Aligning to the Win-Win Playground

Start with finding a quiet place to sit with your feet on the ground.

Close your eyes and bring your focus to your breath. Allow thoughts to emerge and pass through without attachment until you can keep your awareness more steadily on your breath with a quite mind.

Now say silently to yourself: "It is possible for my thoughts, emotions and actions to support my highest good and the highest good of the whole." Stay with this thought as long as it feels right for you.

As you begin to notice changes in your energy field and body, simply be with them without attachment, gently returning your awareness again and again to your breath.

Remain with this process until you experience a sense of completion.

A Meditation to Support Connecting More Deeply to Your Core Essence

I like to do this meditation as a walking meditation, but it can also be done while sitting.

Bring your fingertips of both hands to the point on your abdomen midway between your belly button and the top of your pubic bone. Invite your awareness to float inward to the energetic center of your core essence.

Invite the sparkling golden light of your core essence located at the center of your gravitational body to emerge in your awareness.

Invite your awareness of self to broaden, so you can connect to the radiance of your core essence in every cell and molecule in your body.

As you walk or sit quietly, allow your core essence to communicate with you.

***

Our core essence may communicate through words—for example, "I am kindness," or "I am boundless curiosity." It may also communicate through music, colors, sensations, or a feeling of energized, balanced flow. If you find yourself hearing messages from your judgmental mind, gently bring your awareness to your fingertips with love and then back to the energetic center of your core essence.

I am an early riser. When traveling, I will often get up early, meditate, and then go for a walk as the sun begins to rise. I was once doing my core essence walk in an unfamiliar city when I saw two figures dressed all in black approaching me. Because it was still dim outside, I could not make out their features, and the vagueness of the dark silhouettes briefly activated a fear response in my nervous system.

I had a choice. I could turn around and walk away, or I could look for their core essence. I chose the later. Their core essence was so bright and beautiful. I took a long out-breath to reset my nervous system and continued walking with my awareness on both my core essence and theirs. As they approached, I realized they were an elderly couple each dressed in black coats, pants and hats. No danger—just love. It turned out they were walking the same circular path as I was, only in the opposite direction. I met them again after the sun had fully risen. We laughed and nodded to each other as we passed one another a second time.

The Evolution of Our Self Awareness

Throughout this book, I have spoken about connecting to your higher self, inner wisdom, inner physician, and core essence to help guide decisions that are right for you, and to help you check in with the statement: *This is for my highest good and the for the highest good of the whole.*

When we are checking in with ourselves around an important decision, it is important to be aware of the parts of self that can emerge as the primary decision-makers in our lives. A few of these include the rational or mental self, the emotional self, the wounded or adapted child self, the wise adult self, the higher or spiritual self, and the physical self. We also have archetypal selves that come in as decision makers such as the hero self, the ideal parent self, and the natural child self.

Each of us has habitual ways of relating to ourselves. Part of our evolution involves letting go of externally influenced ideas of who we think we should be and moving towards our authentic selves with loving kindness.

In Gestalt theory, these many parts exist together within the wholeness of who we are. A key tenet of Gestalt theory is that the whole is different from the sum of its parts. As these parts come together in relationship, meaning emerges through the quality of their connection. As aspects of ourselves shift from isolation to connection, our personal energetic field evolves from distortion toward greater coherence.

As we hold these parts in loving connection, they are able to collaborate and take turns leading in healthy ways. Our hero self comes on line when needed in emergencies. Our wise adult self helps us pay our bills on time and engage in deep, caring conversations. Our natural child gets to play during times of rest and joy.

And when our adapted child comes to the forefront—wanting to control, people-please, or hide away—we have the opportunity to re-parent ourselves through the loving presence of our wise adult self. Our adapted child no longer feels alone. It can be honored, supported, and loved without needing to run our lives.

***

Take a moment now to hold all these parts of yourself in loving awareness and connection. There are no rigid rules about how you are supposed to be with yourself. Our parts come together to create the whole of who we are, and how they interact in a healthy way is deeply individual.

I encourage you to become curious about these parts of yourself, as well as the aspect of you that is broader than the sum of your parts. When a part of yourself is in separation, it is often stuck on a younger timeline and may be operating from survival patterns. Because of this, it may continue looking outward for safety and fail to recognize that while it has been vigilantly protecting you from it's child perspective, you have become a wise adult.

Talk to these younger parts of yourself. Invite them to look inward at who you are now. Invite them back into the community of you. Let them know that you are capable, wise, and able to discern whether you are safe. The energy you have put into your survival patterns is your energy, reclaim it for your good. Ask these parts what roles they would like to play in your life now that it no longer need to focus on keeping you safe. Perhaps one part wants to remind you to have fun. Another may want to support your creativity. The possibilities are infinite and deeply personal.

As we connect more with our golden shadow; allowing our core essence to emerge, we gain the opportunity to shift our habitual ways of relating to ourselves. We deepen our relationship to the parts of ourselves that are serving us well and discover the new ways of being that are right for us from a place of deep wisdom and connection.

Using Our Bodies to Signal Alignment

Our journey to connect with ourselves with kindness and clarity is exactly that—a journey. There are many ways to check whether a decision aligns with our highest good and the highest good of the whole. Through years of experience, I have found that it is especially helpful to check in with your body wisdom for the clearest message.

Since we have been exploring how the chakra system effects the personal energy field throughout this book, I will now describe a way to use that system's influence on one's balance. This tool helps keep your actions aligned with the Win-Win Playground.

Start in standing. Rock gently forward and back, then side to side, until you connect to your center.

Now reinforce your center with the words: *It is my intention to align to the Win-Win Playground.* Repeat these words silently to yourself as many times as feels right to you.

Notice the increase in both your sense of groundedness in the present moment and the flow of energy along the energetic intentional line that runs up and down your spine. You may also notice your spine becoming more centered and supple.

Now lets explore the Competitive playground: Say forcefully: *Let my Will be done.* Notice the shift in balance that occurs as you say this. Most of you will tilt forward as your back chakras enlarge.

Return to your center with the words: *It is my intention to align to the Win-Win Playground.*

We move into the Masochist playground when we forget about ourselves and put others needs before our own from the one-down sense that this is how we become lovable. When you say aloud or internally: *Let your will be done* in situations where you are forgetting about yourself, your balance will likely move backwards. You are making decisions from an emotional level which enlarges the front chakras and pushes you backwards.

Realign now to the Win-Win Playground, and to the part of you that is whole, healthy and knows what is best for your highest good and the highest good of the whole.

Let's put the concept of using the balance system into broader practice. Take a moment to think of a decision that has been weighing on you. While noticing your balance, make the statement: "It is for my highest good and the highest good of the whole to....(add your statement here)." Notice your balance as you make the statement. A centered alignment will be a yes. Moving out of center with either part of the statements *It is for my highest good* or *It for the highest good of the whole* will be a clear no.

You can play with your statements. Be as specific as possible. You may need to state your sentences slowly to notice whether there is increased centering or a subtle shift out of balance. Also remember that our body shows us what is right in the moment, so answers can change if something even better emerges for us. Keep yourself open to the possibility that something even better may be just over the horizon, waiting for you to notice it.

Have fun with this! The practice of checking in with yourself becomes easier and more natural over time.

The Power of Breathing

When we find ourselves reliving past trauma, we can breathe ourselves back into the present more easily when we consciously hold ourselves in a container of love and equal connection to Heaven and Earth. Most traumas still held in our body occurred during an experience of fear, overwhelm, powerlessness, or isolation. When we re-experience those memories surrounded by love instead of fear — with agency expressed through our breath, and connection instead of separation—it becomes easier to use breath as a tool for change.

As you begin to breathe deeply and slowly, invite all activated body consciousness to return to present time. You might say to your body:

I am safe. It is now. Come join me in the now.

Continue breathing as the softening in your tissues integrates. Allow your exhale to be two seconds longer than your inhale. This simple adjustment helps reset the nervous system out of its freeze pattern and into a calm parasympathetic—rest and digest—state.

When we notice anxiety about the future or find ourselves stuck in over-planning mode, we can also breathe ourselves back into the present.

While traveling in India several years ago, I was introduced to the concept of focusing on the *next right action*. That practice—along with keeping a simple to-do journal for my various projects—has been profoundly helpful in calming my overactive executive functioning.

There is something deeply grounding about checking in with a list, discerning the next right action, and giving that single task your full attention. It creates a sense of presence and steadiness that supports clarity rather than overwhelm.

As you do this practice, you can also decide how you want to *feel*—safe, competent, joyful, energized—as you do the next right action. The list is endless.

Breathing Ourselves Back to Center

When we slip into one-down consciousness—believing that others are more important than we are—we can breathe ourselves back up to the level playing field of the Win-Win Playground. With each breath, set the intention to reconnect as an equal member of the divine matrix of love.

The golden light of your core essence came here to play. It plays through creativity, connection, and service—through honoring both your own essence and the essence of others.

When we notice ourselves engaging in service that feeds one of the maladaptive playgrounds—the Masochist, the Competitive, or the Human Grenade—we simply pause.

Set the intention to return to the Win-Win Playground.

Take a slow breath.

As you breathe, allow our tissues to soften.

Let your armor release.

Invision yourself fully supported by love and open to receive in a heart centered and balanced way.

Let spaciousness emerge and your perception widen so Plan B can unfold.

As we open to possibilities beyond what we previously believed was possible, we step into the field of miracles—and beautiful things begin to unfold within us and around us.

In my own personal process work, I discovered that one of the greatest constricting forces keeping me from living fully in the field of miracles has been difficulty forgiving myself—for what I did, and for what I failed to do.

Now that I am aware of this pattern, when stuck guilt arises, I return to my Ho'oponopono practice and spend extra time breathing in the energy of:

I forgive myself.

Guilt itself is not the problem. Healthy guilt has a warmth to it. It nudges us to assess ourselves honestly. It invites repair. It says, *You can do better*. And we respond.

But when guilt becomes sharp, barbed, and unresolved, it is often rooted in a deeper belief: *I am bad.*

It doesn't say, "You made a mistake." It says, "You are the mistake."

It is that belief—not guilt itself—that creates what is called false guilt. False guilt does not invite repair. It contracts. It fixes identity. It keeps the nervous system activated. It hardens the field.

I can feel the difference in my own tissues. Healthy guilt softens once I take responsibility. It is *I am sad and I feel remorse for what I have done.* I see the impact my actions have on others and I am called to make a repair. False guilt tightens my diaphragm. It pulls my shoulders forward. It makes my breath shallow. It keeps the nervous system on alert, as if punishment is coming. It happens when I self shame or when I take over-responsibility for someone else's emotions.

Over time, living inside the belief *I am bad* alters the integrity of the personal energy field. It constricts flow. And constricted flow, sustained over years, can contribute to patterns of dis-ease.

This is why forgiveness is not indulgent.

It is structural.

During the COVID shutdown, I spent years in meditation breathing in forgiveness and sending it outward across the Earth—honoring the harm our materialist behaviors have inflicted on the planet. One day, the planet let me know her process with me was complete—that she did not need my help in that way anymore. I trust others to continue the vital work of policy development, systems change, and environmental stewardship. To those of you working in environmental justice: I deeply honor your efforts. When you feel the urge to change your path, honor what comes to you. There are times in our lives in which we are called to look for problems and fix them and there are times in which we are supposed to follow our bliss—honor your patterns, and honor the pause between these inward and outward callings.

When we find ourselves in a one-up position—viewing others through judgment or separation—we once again return to breath and intention.

Take a deep breath. Reconnect to equal footing within the field of Love and Freedom that surrounds us all.

You may silently say:

I am returning to my heart to return to the Win-Win Playground.

If you are highly activated, remember to lengthen your exhale by two seconds to help your system settle.

Breath is always available. It is the bridge back to presence. It is the doorway to choice. And it is one of the most powerful tools we have for returning—again and again—to love.

The Win-Win Breath

Use this anytime you feel overwhelmed, disconnected, judgmental, depleted, or stuck.

1. Pause. Soften your gaze.

2. Inhale slowly through your nose for a count of four.

3. Exhale gently for a count of six—two seconds longer than the inhale.

4. Repeat for three to five breaths.

5. Set your intention silently or aloud: I am returning to the Win-Win Playground.

As you breathe, allow your tissues to soften and your awareness to widen. Notice what shifts. Trust that the next right action will emerge.

Breath is the simplest bridge back to presence, back to choice, and back to love. When we use breath consciously in the field of love, we return to heart-centered connection and regain access to the Win-Win Playground. Through breath, we soften fixation, release separation, and allow Grace to reveal what comes next. Again and again, breath invites us home—to ourselves, to each other, and to the field of Love and Freedom that holds us all.

The Power of Your Words

Here is a summary of the affirmations and anchor phrases used in this book:

To support becoming a co-creator with the Divine, ask:

"How can I support my life—and the lives of those around me—to be even more amazing than they already are?"

To open to spaciousness in your tissues and the flow of Grace in your life, as you visualize spaciousness increasing in your body, state:

"Let Thy will be done."

To support showing up in love:

"I invite my energy field into centered alignment and balanced receiving of love."

We integrate this statement energetically by saying:

"I am setting the intention to align to my highest good and the highest good of the whole."

We invite ease of positive flow into our lives by saying:

"I am opening to the possibility of being in ease and positive flow with my creative projects."

To detach from a specific outcome, add to your image of the future:

"...or something even better."

To open to the possibility of stepping into the Win-Win Playground:

"I open to the possibility of living more fully in the Win-Win Playground." And

"I open to the possibility that all my needs, and the needs of those around me are supported with ease".

To feed the positive energies of the Win-Win Playground and open yourself to curiosity ask: **"What is missing?"** and **"How can I support my life** *and* **the lives of those around me to be even more amazing than they already are?"**

To check in on a decision: **"This is for my highest good and the highest good of the whole."**

To support the habit of checking in with self before jumping up to help others, ask:

"Do I actually have the capacity for this right now? "

And ask if you find yourself getting depleted:

"Is this mine to do?" and **"Is this mine to do now?"**

When you feel one down and walled off, return to equal footing:

"It is possible to be an equal member of the divine, and an equal player on the Win-Win Playground."

When you feel one down and depleted, open to receiving. First give yourself permission to feed yourself:

"It is okay to receive more than I give."

As your capacity to hold larger and larger amounts of energy increases:

"I am filling myself with the balanced energy of love from heaven and earth to meet all my needs and the needs of those around me for today equally."

When you notice people-pleasing (one down and depleting):

"I am safe. I am an equal member of God's team. My needs are equally important to the needs of the whole."

When you find yourself one-down and walled off:

"I am filling myself with the balanced energy of love from heaven and earth to support all my needs and the needs of those around me for today. I am an equal member of God's team."

To invite all activated body consciousness to return to present time. You can say:

"I am safe, I am surrounded by love, it is now, come join me in the now."

To support having a healthier container around money say:

"It is okay to receive more money than I give."

To support loving neutrality around money:

"Money is energy, and energy is love."

Whether you are in a depletion pattern or a hoarding pattern around money—to support increasing healthy flow—ask:

"What subtle but profound changes can I make to be in healthier relationship to the flow of money?"

To support building a healthy and balanced container for receiving love and abundance, tune into both Heaven and Earth and say:

"I have loving and abundant Parents."

When you notice you are taking on other's issues energetically or physically, you can say:

"I am releasing all patterns that are not mine to do."

When you notice yourself going one up, return to equality:

**"The love in you is as important as the love in me. We are

all God's children. We all deserve to play on the Win-Win Playground."

When you notice you are over focused on a project and neglecting those around you, bring your energy back to your heart. You can say:

"I am co-creating this project with Love. I feel Love's support. Love is the energy that will bring the positive change."

Or:

"I choose to co-create from love. My passion is supported by grace. I can act on what I love with full connection to the equal playing field."

When you find yourself in deep disconnection ask yourself:

"Are my actions being fed by love or fear?"

When you feel hopeless or overly attached to outcome, soften and return to receiving:

"I am softening my armor and allowing grace to enter my cells to create the Plan B in my life that is even better than what I can currently imagine. I attune to the love of heaven"

and earth to support all my needs and the needs of those around me equally."

Walking in the Win-Win Playground:

"I am blessed. I and everyone around me have exactly what we need."

Traditional Ho'oponopono prayer:

"I love you. I am sorry. Please forgive me. Thank you."

The version of Ho'oponopono I currently use:

"I love me. I honor what is here, now, in my tissues. I am sorry. I forgive me. I am grateful for the lesson."

To explore dampened creative instincts, ask:

"Was there anything I loved to do as a child that was dampened by my life experiences?"

To support your creative projects to remain in the Win-Win playground, you can ask:

"How might engaging in this creative project make my life, and the lives of those around me even more wonderful?"

During stressful situations, instead of blaming self or others, return to agency and curiosity by saying:

"This is for me. What is here for me to learn?"

Divine Timing in Action

I began 2026 in the hospital, recovering from renal failure and major abdominal surgery following a ruptured colon. I was facing a temporary colostomy and the realities that came with it, while also standing at the threshold of what I had imagined would be the beginning of retirement.

What fascinated me was how precisely timed everything was. Despite my condition, I did not need to cancel my forty-day journey to South America and Antarctica scheduled for the end of February. Before placing the deposit for this trip, I checked in deeply:

I made the following statement while listening to my body's reaction of expansion or contraction.

It is for my highest good and the highest good of all to spend forty days in South America and Antarctica starting at the end of February 2026.

The response was a strong yes—and it remains so. At the time of this book being published, I have successfully travelled to Argentina, the Falkland Islands, South Georgia, Antarctica and cruised the Chilean Fiords. I stood in a field of 200,000 king penguins on the

Salisbury Plain in South Georgia, walked around hundreds of fur seals, kayaked next to a sleeping whale, and saw an iceberg form from the calving of the six km wide Pio XI glacier in Chile. During this time, I had wonderful conversations, ate wonderful food, and was supported by the staff of the cruise line in so many ways. Now that I am retired, it is my soul's desire to celebrate the wonders of the planet, and I am doing that.

During my thirteen-day hospital stay, I had four roommates. Each one taught me something essential about life.

The first showed me a functional model of interdependence. She was fifty-five, like me, and had lived her whole life with severe asthma and diabetes. She cared for her mother, and one of her sons lived with and cared for her. Watching her interaction softened my gaze and loosened fixations I had been holding about my own adult son who lives with us.

My second roommate was eighty-three and had recently married a ninety-year-old man. They laughed constantly. Their intimacy and joy moved me deeply, and one night I lay in bed grateful that my own husband made me smile every time he entered the room.

The third roommate was a twenty-six-year-old special education teacher with Crohn's disease. She discovered she was pregnant when she went into surgery after being told she might never be able to have children. She reminded me of miracles. I reminded her of the resilience of human life, inviting her to hold a protective golden dome of love around her baby as she healed.

My final roommate, Norma, was traveling to visit family for the holidays when she experienced a sudden flare of sickle cell disease. A woman from the South, she sang gospel music throughout the day, including a refrain close to:

May I be blessed, so that everyone around me has exactly what they need.

As I walked the hospital halls each day connected to IV antibiotics, I played with the energy of those words until something settled deeply in my body:

I am blessed. I and everyone around me have exactly what we need.

I repeated these words silently as I walked, feeling the vibration move through me and outward toward the staff and patients on my floor. What could have been dreary and monotonous became infused with meaning—and even joy.

Despite my health challenges, I was playing in the Win-Win Playground.

Conclusion
Choosing the Win-Win Playground

This book has been an invitation.

Not an invitation to become perfect. Not an invitation to "fix" yourself. But an invitation to remember who you already are—and to choose, again and again, the playground that nourishes both you and the whole.

The six habits you have explored are not linear steps. They are living practices that interact with one another, strengthening and deepening over time. Each habit supports the others, creating a resilient inner system that helps you return to alignment whenever life pulls you off center.

Healthy Habit #1 invited you to soften your gaze, show up in love, and let go of outcome. This habit opens the doorway. It loosens fixation and helps you receive the Plan B that God is continually offering—a plan often more expansive than anything our conditioned mind could design.

Healthy Habit #2 asked you to consciously align with the Win-Win Playground. This is the orientation point. When both you and the whole matter equally, health, creativity, and service begin to flow together rather than compete.

Healthy Habit #3 reminded you that your state of being matters. When you choose love, acceptance, forgiveness, and gratitude—especially toward yourself—you become a beacon of light simply by being present. The world responds not to your effort, but to your alignment.

Healthy Habit #4 brought you back to creativity—not as performance or productivity, but as a natural expression of life force. Creativity reconnects you to wonder, curiosity, and joy. It restores flow and keeps your nervous system flexible rather than defended.

Healthy Habit #5 invited you to stay curious about the complexities of the human experience. Curiosity keeps you out of blame and false certainty. It allows healing to unfold in layered, multidimensional ways, honoring body wisdom, lineage, environment, and soul timing.

Healthy Habit #6 called you to go to the Source—to step into direct relationship with what is true beneath symptoms, stories, and roles. It is here that involution and evolution meet: your inner knowing and God's grace working together to reveal the next right step.

Practiced together, these habits create a self-correcting system.

When you notice yourself slipping into over-giving, judgment, fear, or collapse, one habit naturally leads you back to another. You soften. You breathe. You realign. You choose again.

Life will continue to challenge you. There will be moments when you find yourself in the Masochist Playground, the Competitive Playground, or even the Human Grenade Playground. That does not mean you have failed. It means you are human.

What matters is not where you land—but how quickly, gently, and compassionately you return.

Each time you choose the Win-Win Playground, you strengthen your capacity to stay there longer. Your nervous system learns safety. Your body learns trust. Your creativity expands. Your service becomes sustainable. And your life becomes a clearer expression of love in action.

You do not walk this path alone.

When you choose the Win-Win Playground, you join a growing field of people who are remembering how to live in alignment with love, freedom, and grace. Your choice matters. Your presence matters. Your healing ripples outward in ways you may never fully see.

So when you feel unsure, overwhelmed, or disconnected, return to the simplest truth:

Soften your gaze. Breathe. Choose love. Let go of outcome. And step back into the playground where everyone—yourself included—has exactly what they need.

You can choose again.

And again.

The playground is still open.

The habits are not steps. They are movements—available in any order.

A Final Affirmation

I soften my gaze and return to love.

I release attachment to outcome and trust divine timing.

I choose the Win-Win Playground—where my needs and the needs of the whole matter equally.

I am open to creativity, curiosity, and grace.

I listen to my body wisdom.

I honor my inner guidance.

When I forget, I remember again.

When I contract, I breathe and expand.

When I stumble, I forgive myself and return to love.

I am a beacon of light—not by what I do, but by how I choose to be.

I am supported.

I am guided.

I am enough.

May I be blessed, so that I, and everyone around me, has exactly what we need.

And so it is.

About the Author

Sarah Day is a facilitator of healing whose work bridges somatic practice, group process, and spiritual inquiry. Her path in the healing arts began in high school, working with young adults with autism—an experience that shaped her lifelong commitment to honoring each person's innate wisdom and capacity for healing.

For over thirty years, Sarah worked as a Pediatric Occupational Therapist, specializing in CranioSacral Therapy, Reflex Integration, and Somatic Experiencing. Her clinical work has consistently focused on supporting nervous system regulation, embodied awareness, and sustainable healing that arises from within rather than being imposed from the outside.

A lifelong learner, Sarah is currently studying with the Barbara Brennan School of Healing. She serves as a Primary Therapist with the Upledger Comprehensive Therapy Programs and the Dolphin-Accompanied Therapy Programs in the Bahamas through Integrative Intentions. These immersive, multi-hands group healing environments reflect her deep belief in the power of collective, heart-centered facilitation.

Sarah is also a co-owner of Poiesis House LLC, a center for self-discovery and healing in Truth or Consequences, New Mexico. Poiesis House supports Advanced-level CranioSacral Therapy training through the Upledger Institute and offers ongoing Advanced Retreats for therapists who have completed the advanced curriculum. The center is currently expanding to provide group healing programs for the general public.

In addition to her clinical and teaching work, Sarah founded Win-Win Playground Press, a publishing imprint dedicated to books that support living in deeper connection to self, God's will, grace, and love. Twenty percent of all profits from books published through the press are donated to the Win-Win Playground Foundation, on whose board Sarah serves. The Foundation's mission is to support the training of therapists in loving, group-based healing environments and to increase public access to group healing experiences that honor each individual's connection to their deep, authentic self as the true source of healing—revealed in right timing and in the right way.

Sarah lives in New Mexico, where she continues to facilitate group healing programs, teach, write, and co-create spaces that invite curiosity, creativity, and embodied connection.

Ways to Give Back

By purchasing this book, you have already given back. Twenty percent of net profits from this book are donated to the Win-Win Playground Foundation. No other action is needed. The purpose of the Win-Win Playground Foundation is to increase access to group healing programs that support connecting in not out, to find the new way.

If you feel inspired to support the Foundation even more, please consider purchasing merchandise from the Win-Win Playground store. One hundred percent of profits from the store are donated to the Win-Win Playground Foundation.

If you would like to support more people in accessing multi-hands facilitated craniosacral therapy programs in the broader Upledger community, please reach out to Upledger International Foundation at www.upledger.com.

If you would like to sponsor a student to study with the Barbara Brennan School of Healing, please visit barbarabrennan.com, click Request Information, and contact the school about sponsoring a student.

Sarah is a co-owner of Poiesis House LLC, a center for self-discovery and healing in Truth or Consequences, New Mexico. Poiesis House supports Advanced-level CranioSacral Therapy training through the Upledger Institute and offers ongoing Advanced Retreats for therapists who have completed the advanced curriculum. The center is currently expanding to provide group healing programs for the general public.

If you would like to experience the healing matrix of Poiesis House without attending an Advanced CranioSacral class or retreat, you can rent the house on Airbnb here: www.airbnb.com/h/poiesis

With thanks,

Sarah Day

Bibliography

Assagioli, Robert. Psychosynthesis. Viking Press, 1965.

Brennan, Barbara. Hands of Light: A Guide to Healing Through the Human Energy Field. Bantam, 1987.

Brennan, Barbara. Light Emerging: The Journey of Personal Healing. Bantam, 1993.

Brennan, Barbara. Core Light Healing: My Personal Journey and Advanced Healing Concepts for Creating the Life You Long to Live. Hay House Inc., 2022.

Brown, Brené. The Gifts of Imperfection. Hazelden Publishing, 2010.

Brown, Brené. Daring Greatly: How the Courage to Be Vulnerable Transforms the Way We Live, Love, Parent, and Lead. Gotham Books, 2012.

Campbell, Joseph. On Bliss. New World Library, 1991.

Dennison, Paul E. Brain Gym and Me: Reclaiming the Pleasure of

Learning. Edu-Kinesthetics, 1988.

Dickens, Ky. The Telepathy Tapes Podcast. Season 1, Episode 9.

Eden, Donna. Eye Health Routine. Workshop Handout, Donna Eden Medicine, Year 1, 2009.

Hay, Louise. Heal Your Body: A Manual for Mind and Body. Hay House, 1976.

Hay, Louise. You Can Heal Your Life. Hay House, 1984.

Harris, Lee, Pam Gregory. A Major Energy Shift is Coming for Lightworkers. LeeHarrisEnergy youtube video. January 2026

The Holy Bible. New International Version, HarperCollins, 2011.

Jung, Carl. Collected Works of C. G. Jung. Edited by Sir Herbert Read et al., Princeton University Press, 1953–1979.

Klotz, Neil-Douglas. Revelations of the Aramaic Jesus. Hampton Roads Books, 2022.

Lerner, Harriet PhD. Why won't you apologize? Healing Big Betrayals and Everyday Hurts. Simon & Shuster, 2017

Levine, Peter A. Waking the Tiger: Healing Trauma — The Innate Capacity to Transform Overwhelming Experiences. North Atlantic Books, 1997.

Levine, Peter A. In an Unspoken Voice: How the Body Releases Trauma and Restores Goodness. North Atlantic Books, 2010.

Machiavelli, Niccoli. The Prince. Originally published 1532. Translated by W.K. Marriott. Polis and Praxis Press,2025.

Nestor, James. Breath: The New Science of a Lost Art. Riverhead Books, 2020.

Pew Research Center. As Partisan Hostility Grows, Signs of Frustration With the Two-Party System. https://www.pewresearch.org/wp-content/uploads/sites/2 0/2022/08/PP_2022.09.08_partisan-hostility_REPORT.pdf

Perls, Frederick S. M.D, PhD. Gestalt Therapy Verbatim: An action approach to deepening awareness and living fully in the Here and Now, as experienced in workshops at Esalen Institute. 2nd Ed. The Gestalt Institute Press. 2013.

Real, Terry. The New Rules of Marriage: What You Need to Know to Make Love Work. Ballantine Books, 2007.

Real, Terry. Us: Getting Past You and Me to Build a More Loving Relationship. Rodale Books, 2022.

Rilke, Rainer Maria. Letters to a Young Poet. Warbler Press edition, 2022.

Rudd, Richard. Gene Keys: Unlocking The Higher Purpose Hidden In Your DNA 3rd Edition. Gene Keys Publishing, 2015.

Schwartz, Richard, C and Sweezy, M. Internal Family Systems Therapy, Second Edition. The Guildford Press, 2020.

Shinn, Florence Scovel. The Game of Life and How to Play It. T. S. Allen, 1925.

Tolle, Eckhart. The Power of Now: A Guide to Spiritual Enlightenment. Namaste Publishing, 1997; republished by New World Library, 1999.

Upledger, John E. Your Inner Physician and You. North Atlantic Books, 1984.

Upledger, John E. Somato-Emotional Release and Beyond. North Atlantic Books, 1996.

van der Kolk, Bessel. M.D. The Body Keeps the Score: Brain, Mind and Body in the Healing of Trauma. Penguin Books, 2015.

Wilkerson, Isabel. Caste: The Origins of Our Discontents. Random House, 2020.

www.ingramcontent.com/pod-product-compliance
Lightning Source LLC
Chambersburg PA
CBHW032018150726
47990CB00005B/2015